T5-AVQ-445

VAULT CAREER GUIDE TO INVESTMENT MANAGEMENT

who benefits most
from your hard work?

That's the question that makes many people consider working for themselves. The freedoms of self-employment offer great choices that affect the quality of your life and the lives of others. You choose with whom you want to work and the level of success to which you aspire. With hard work, your income can be a reflection of your energy, commitment and drive—not someone else's expectations.

With 145 years of industry experience, Northwestern Mutual understands the importance of its Financial Representatives making the right self-employment choices—because success begins with choosing the path that's right for you.

Take the online Self-Employment Screen and explore the opportunities that are most suitable to your personality. Log on to http://careers.nmfn.com and explore "Begin Now."

Send resume to:
resume@northwesternmutual.com

Northwestern Mutual
FINANCIAL NETWORK®

Are you there yet?®

www.nmfn.com

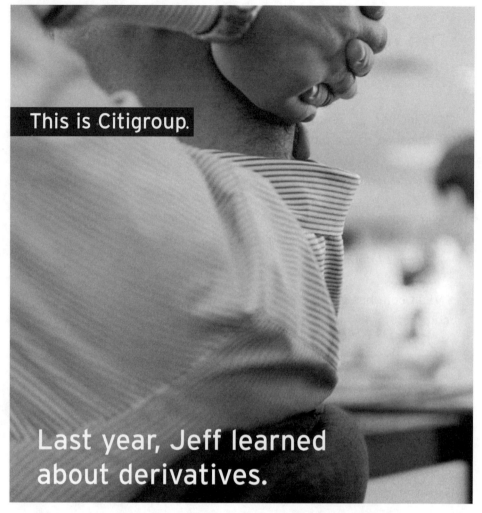

This is Citigroup.

Last year, Jeff learned about derivatives.

This year, he traded $200 Million worth of them.

During a course in investments, something "clicked"–Jeff knew he wanted to become a derivatives trader. A year later, he was helping to conduct some of the biggest trades in the world. Jeff believes this could have only happened at Citigroup. With a revolutionary business model that is quickly changing the industry, Citigroup recruits ambitious, highly talented people and allows them to find their own path to their potential. To find out more, come to one of our on-campus presentations or have a look online. Who knows? It could be one of the best investments you'll ever make. **Citigroup.com**

Salomon Smith Barney & Citibank

VAULT CAREER GUIDE TO INVESTMENT MANAGEMENT

ANDREW SCHLOSSBERG
WITH ALEXANDER GORELIK
AND THE STAFF OF VAULT

Library of Congress CIP Data is available.

ISBN 1-58131-179-6

Printed in the United States of America

ACKNOWLEDGEMENTS

Andrew Schlossberg would like to thank his wife Lauren: "For your patience, encouragement, and support."

Vault would like to acknowledge the assistance and support of Matt Doull, Ahmad Al-Khaled, Lee Black, Eric Ober, Hollinger Ventures, Tekbanc, New York City Investment Fund, American Lawyer Media, Globix, Hoover's, Glenn Fischer, Mark Hernandez, Ravi Mhatre, Carter Weiss, Ken Cron, Ed Somekh, Isidore Mayrock, Zahi Khouri, Sana Sabbagh and other Vault investors. Many thanks to our loving families and friends.

Special thanks to Deborah Adeyanju and Evan Cohen. Thanks also to H.S. Hamadeh, Derek Loosvelt, Val Hadjiyski, Marcy Lerner, Chris Prior, Rob Schipano, Ed Shen, and Tyya N. Turner and the rest of the Vault staff for their support.

Applying for Business school?

Taking the **GMAT*** ?

Short on time to prepare?
Want more than "tricks?"

Manhattan GMAT*

The new standard in GMAT test-prep.
Designed for students applying to top schools -
who need top scores on the test.

· Nine-week advanced course with free homework help
· Private/custom instruction and online tutoring

150 West 25th Street, 10th floor

Join the experts at NYC's only test
prep firm dedicated solely to the
GMAT.

For more information or to register,
call **212-721-7400**
or visit **www.manhattangmat.com**

Too busy
signing on the dotted line
to sign off on your
new ski chalet?

Table of Contents

INTRODUCTION   1

    History 2
    The Industry Today 5

THE SCOOP   3

Buy-side vs. Sell-side   11
    Jobs on the Buy-side 12
    Jobs on the Sell-side 15
    Recommended Reading 18

The Clients of Asset Managers   21
    Mutual Funds 22
    Institutional Investors 25
    High Net Worth 29

Investment Styles   33
    Type of Security 34
    Risk Characteristics of Investments .35
    Portfolio Construction 39
    Summary of Investment Styles 41
    How Is This Relevant to My Job Search? 42

ON THE JOB

Portfolio Management   45
    The Three Segments 45
    Senior Portfolio Manager 46
    Associate Portfolio Manager 47
    Portfolio Manager Assistant 48

Investment Research   51

Senior Research Analyst 51

Investment Research Associate 52

Investment Research Assistant 53

Marketing and Sales   55

Marketing and Sales Manager 55

Marketing Associate 56

Alternative Entry Points 57

Days in the Life   59

Investment Research Associate, Major Mutual Fund Firm 59

Investment Management Associate, J.P. Morgan Fleming 61

Investment Banking Research Associate,
Deutsche Bank Equity Research 62

Investment Banking Equity Research Associate,
Salomon Smith Barney 64

GETTING HIRED

Targeting Your Job Search   69

Getting the Interview 69

Who are the Asset Management Employers? A Basic Breakdown 71

Who are the Asset Management Employers? A Closer Look 73

Venture Capital Funds and Hedge Funds 79

Is This Firm Right for Me? 80

The Interview   83

Preparing for the Interview 83

Background Questions 64

Stock and Bond Recommendations and Valuation Questions 86

Economic Questions 90

Financial Accounting Questions 91

Personality/Fit Questions 93

APPENDIX

Investment Management Glossary   97

Valuing a Company   105

Ratio Analysis 105

Discounted Cash Flow (DCF Analysis) 107

About the Authors   109

Introduction

How many industries can you think of that impact households all over the world? Very few. That is one of the many exciting aspects of the asset management industry – more people than ever before are planning for their future financial needs, and as a result, the industry is more visible and important than ever.

The asset management community seeks to preserve and grow capital for individuals and institutional investors alike. This Vault Career Guide will serve as an insider guide for careers in the industry. It will provide you with the knowledge to appropriately target your career search and a framework to handle the most challenging interviews.

Investment Management vs. Asset Management

A quick note about the terms **investment management** and **asset management**: these terms are often used interchangeably. They refer to the same practice – the professional management of assets through investment. Investment management is used a bit more often when referring to the activity or career (i.e., "I'm an investment manager" or "That firm is gaining a lot of business in investment management"), whereas "asset management" is used more with reference to the industry itself (i.e., "The asset management industry").

More stability

Because of the stability of cash flows generated by the industry, investment management provides a relatively stable career when compared to some other financial services positions (most notably investment banking). Investment management firms are generally paid a set fee as a percentage of assets under management. (The fee structure varies, and sometimes is both an asset-centered fee plus a performance fee, especially for institutional investors.) Still, even when investment management fees involve a performance incentive, the business is much less cyclical than cousins like investment banking. Banking fees depend on transactions. When banking activities such as IPOs and M&A transactions dry up, so do fees for investment banks, which translates into layoffs of bankers. In contrast, assets are quite simply always being invested.

History

To better understand why asset management has become such a critical component of the broader financial services industry, we must first become acquainted with its formation and history.

The beginnings of a separate industry

While the informal process of managing money has been around since the beginning of the 20th century, the industry did not begin to mature until the early 1970's. Prior to that time, investment management was completely relationship-based. Assignments to manage assets grew out of relationships that banks and insurance companies already had with institutions – primarily companies or municipal organizations with employee pension funds – that had funds to invest. (A pension fund is set up as an employee benefit. Employers commit to a certain level of payment to retired employees each year and must manage their funds to meet these obligations. Organizations with large pools of assets to invest are called institutional investors.)

These asset managers were chosen in an unstructured way – assignments grew organically out of pre-existing relationships, rather than through a formal request for proposal and bidding process. The actual practice of investment management was also unstructured. At the time, asset managers might simply pick 50 stocks they thought were good investments – there was not nearly as much analysis on managing risk or organizing a fund around a specific category or style. (Examples of different investment categories include small cap stocks and large cap stocks. We will explore the different investment categories and styles in a later chapter.) Finally, the assets that were managed at the time were primarily pension funds. Mutual funds had yet to become broadly popular.

ERISA, 401(k) plans and specialist firms

The two catalysts for change in the industry were: 1) the broad realization that demographic trends would cause the U.S. government's retirement system (Social Security) to be underfunded, which made individuals more concerned with their retirement savings, and 2) the creation of ERISA (the Employment Retirement Income Secruity Act) in 1974, which gave employees incentives to save for retirement privately through 401(k) plans. (401(k) plans allow employees to save pre-tax earnings for their retirement.) These elements prompted an increased focus on long-term savings by individual investors and the formation of what can be described as a private pension fund market.

These fundamental changes created the opportunity for professional groups of money managers to form "specialist" firms to manage individual and institutional assets. Throughout the 1970s and early 1980s, these small firms specialized in one or two investment styles (for example, core equities or fixed income investing).

During this period, the investment industry became fragmented and competitive. This competition added extra dimensions to the asset management industry. Investment skills, of course, remained critical. However, relationship building and the professional presentation of money management teams also began to become significant.

The rise of the mutual fund

In the early to mid 1980s, driven by the ERISA laws, the mutual fund came into vogue. While mutual funds had been around for decades, they were only used by financially sophisticated investors who paid a lot of attention to their investments. However, investor sophistication increased with the advent of modern portfolio theory (the set of tools developed to quantitatively analyze the management of a portfolio; see sidebar on next page). Asset management firms began heavily marketing mutual funds as a safe and smart investment tool, pitching to individual investors the virtues of diversification and other benefits of investing in mutual funds. With more and more employers shifting retirement savings responsibilities from pension funds to the employees themselves, the 401(k) market grew rapidly. Consequently, consumer demand for new mutual fund products exploded (mutual funds are the preferred choice in most 401(k) portfolios). Many specialists responded by expanding their product offerings and focusing more on the marketing of their new services and capabilities.

Modern Portfolio Theory

Modern Portfolio Theory (MPT) was born in 1952 when University of Chicago economics student Harry Markowitz published his doctoral thesis, "Portfolio Selection," in the *Journal of Finance*. Markowitz, who won the Nobel Prize in economics in 1990 for his research and its far-reaching effects, provided the framework for what is now known as Modern Portfolio Theory. MPT quantifies the benefits of diversification, looking at how investors create portfolios in order to optimize market risk against expected returns. Markowitz, assuming all investors are risk averse, proposed that investors, when choosing a security to add to their portfolio, should not base their decision on the amount of risk that an individual security has, but rather on how that security contributes to the overall risk of the portfolio. To do this, Markowitz considered how securities move in relation to one another under similar circumstances. This is called "correlation," which measures how much two securities fluctuate in price relative to each other. Taking all this into account, investors can create "efficient portfolios," ones with the highest expected returns for a given level of risk.

Consolidation and globalization

The dominant themes of the industry in the 1990s were consolidation and globalization. As many former specialists rapidly expanded, brand recognition and advanced distribution channels (through brokers or other sales vehicles) became key success factors for asset management companies. Massive global commercial and investment banks entered the industry, taking business away from many specialist firms. Also, mutual fund rating agencies such as Lipper (founded in 1973, now a part of Reuters) and Morningstar (founded in Chicago in 1984) increased investor awareness of portfolio performance. These rating agencies publish reports on fund performance and rate funds on scales such as Morningstar's 4-star rating system.

These factors led to a shakeout period of consolidation. From 1995 to 2001, approximately 150 mergers took place, creating well-established and formidable players such as Capital Group and Citigroup. As opposed to specialist firms, these large financial services firms provide asset management products that run the gamut: mutual funds, pension funds, management for high-net-worth individuals, etc. While many excellent specialist firms continue to operate today, they are not the driving force that they once were.

The Industry Today

Wealth creation in the 1990s has led to even greater demand for money management services today. In the U.S. alone, 2.8 million families have reached millionaire status. Mutual fund demand has continued to increase; as of 2002, there were 8,000 different funds in the market, up from just 3,000 in 1990. In fact, nearly 50 million households invest in mutual funds, with a total worth of $8.5 trillion, up from only $340 billion in 1984 and $1 trillion as recently as 1990.

As the industry has matured, total assets under management (AUMs) in the United States have grown to $20 trillion. Consolidation and globalization have created a diverse list of leading industry players that range from well-capitalized divisions of investment banks, global insurance companies and multinational commercial banks to independent behemoths, such as Fidelity and Capital Group.

Below is a list of the 20 largest worldwide asset management companies as of 2001. Pay attention to one critical component that may not be immediately obvious: the leading players in the industry are located all over the U.S. Working in the industry, unlike other areas of financial services like investment banking, does not require that you live in a particular region of the country.

Top 20 Firms Ranked by Worldwide Assets Under Management	U.S. Headquarters	AUM's as of 12/31/01 ($ millions)
Fidelity Investments	Boston, MA	$1,007,898
State Street Global	Boston, MA	$784,712
Barclay's Global	San Francisco, CA	$768,700
Deutsche Asset Management	New York, NY	$748,607
Vanguard Group	Valley Forge, PA	$605,556
J.P. Morgan Fleming	New York, NY	$604,660
Merrill Lynch	New York, NY	$528,701
Alliance Capital	New York, NY	$455,404
Citigroup Asset Management	Stamford, CT	$416,881
Morgan Stanley Inv. Management	New York, NY	$415,984
UBS Global Asset Management	Chicago, IL	$400,312
Prudential Financial	Newark, NJ	$387,959
AMVESCAP - AIM and INVESCO	Atlanta, Houston, Denver	$376,112
Capital Research	Los Angeles, CA	$367,055
Northern Trust Global	Chicago, IL	$330,058
Putnam Investments	Boston, MA	$314,566
AIG Global Investment	New York, NY	$312,998
Wellington Management	Boston, MA	$307,212
Goldman Sachs	New York, NY	$306,014
Franklin Templeton	San Mateo, CA	$266,287

Source: Pension and Investments, May 2002

More than just investment

More than ever, asset management companies are focusing on more than just investing. Business decisions such as marketing and distribution, global growth and technology integration are becoming increasingly important factors in the success of investment management firms. While this Guide will focus mainly on developing a career on the investment side of the investment management industry, we will also spend some time discussing the growing alternative career opportunities relating to these "non-investment" business issues.

Find investment management firm profiles, the Vault Investment Management Careers Message board, and open positions in investment management at the Vault Finance Career Channel:

http://finance.vault.com

We also recommend these Vault guides:

- Vault Career Guide to Investment Banking
- Vault Career Guide to Venture Capital
- Vault Career Guide to Accounting
- Vault Guide to Finance Interviews
- Vault Guide to Advanced and Quantitative Finance Interviews

THE SCOOP

Chapter 2: Buy-side vs. Sell-side

Chapter 3: The Clients of Investment Managers

Chapter 4: Investment Styles

Buy-side vs. Sell-side

If you've ever spoken with investment professionals, you've probably heard them talk about the "buy-side" and the "sell-side." What do these terms mean and how do the two sides of the Street interact with one another?

What's the difference?

Simply stated, the buy-side refers to the asset managers who represent individual and institutional investors. The buy-side purchases investment products with the goal of increasing its assets. The sell-side refers to the functions of an investment bank. Specifically, this includes investment bankers, traders and research analysts. Sell-side professionals issue, recommend, trade and "sell" securities for the investors on the buy-side to "buy." The sell-side can be thought of primarily as a facilitator of buy-side investments – the sell-side makes money not through a growth in value of the investment, but through fees and commissions for these facilitating services. In this chapter, we'll take a brief look at the types of jobs on each "side." The rest of the book will look at the buy-side in detail.

Jobs on the Buy-side

Buy-side firms are structured in a far less formal manner than sell-side firms. Consequently, career paths are more flexible and job descriptions vary more from one firm to another. In general, buy-side firms have a three-segment professional staff consisting of:

- Portfolio managers who invest money on behalf of clients
- Research analysts who provide portfolio managers with potential investment recommendations
- Marketing and sales professionals who distribute the investment products to individual and institutional investors

When beginning your career on the buy-side, you typically will start as an assistant or associate in one of these three areas.

Professional Positions in Asset Management

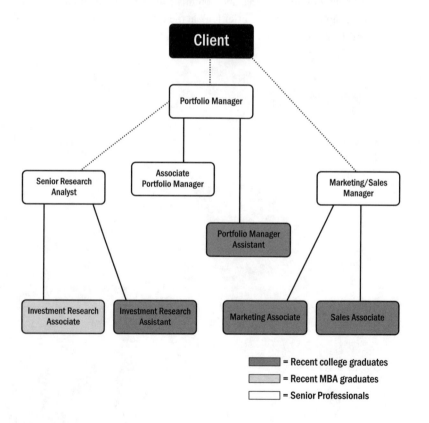

Structure: Buy-side vs. sell-side

In general, investment management companies are less structured than most other types of finance firms, including investment banks, commercial banks and accounting firms. As a result, investment management positions have less-defined job descriptions than positions at other types of finance firms. Job descriptions for similar titles in the investment management industry differ from firm to firm. And only the largest firms in asset management have all of the positions described in this book. That said, when interviewing for investment management positions, you should ask your interviewer to clarify exact job responsibilities. By doing so, you'll not only gain insight into the position, you'll also sound informed about the (lack of) structure in the industry.

Positions for recent college graduates

Recent college graduates typically enter the industry as investment research assistants or portfolio manager assistants. Both positions offer great opportunities to learn the nuances and fundamentals of the business by working directly with senior analysts and portfolio managers.

Investment research assistants maintain investment models, gather industry and company information and help devise recommendations. Investment research assistants support research analysts who focus on particular areas of investment (for example, a number of companies in an industry), rather than specific investment funds.

Portfolio manager assistants screen for potential investments, monitor portfolio characteristics and assist in client relations. Portfolio manager assistants offer support to portfolio managers, who typically oversee specific investment funds (for example, a specific mutual fund or pension fund).

Most people spend two to three years in these positions before seeking an MBA and moving up. On occasion, assistants are promoted directly to investment research associate without an MBA. However, this is rare and tends to occur only at the smaller investment management firms.

Another less traveled route for recent college graduates is to join a firm's marketing and sales department as either a marketing or sales associate, both of which have very similar functions.

Marketing associates assist in creating portfolio review presentations and in developing promotional presentations for potential new clients.

Sales associates assist in answering RFPs (requests for proposals) issued by institutions seeking to hire new investment managers, and assist senior sales officials in maintaining and expanding existing client relationships.

Marketing and sales have become increasingly critical functions in the investment management industry. This path is an outstanding alternative for those interested in the industry but not driven by investing money. Also, a marketing or sales associate role can serve as an entry point to the industry or a springboard to a switch to the investment side. While the duties and functions of sales and marketing associates are very similar, and often overlap, the difference is this: salespeople are responsible for generating new business and maintaining existing client relationships, whereas marketing professionals support the sales effort by (for example) creating the promotional materials that salespeople use to pitch clients and instructing salespeople on how best to pitch a certain product.

Positions for recent MBA graduates

Recent MBA graduates or working professionals with considerable investment experience typically enter the industry as investment research associates. They are usually assigned a small industry to cover, providing them with an opportunity to get their feet wet.

Investment research associates provide insight and investment recommendations to portfolio managers. The typical day includes listening to company management conference calls, attending industry conferences, building investment models, developing industry trends and benchmarking company progress to its peers.

Success as a research associate will lead to advancement to larger industries and ultimately to the role of portfolio manager (a large percentage of portfolio managers rise through the ranks as research analysts).

Jobs on the Sell-side

Because of a relatively larger number of job assignments, as well as higher turnover of staff, the sell-side employs more recent college and business school graduates than the buy-side. For instance, many large investment banks hire upwards of 100 recently minted MBAs and college graduates annually to begin as bankers and research analysts.

Positions in investment banking

Investment banking professionals assist companies in raising capital and exploring various financial alternatives. (Professionals in I-banking are called analysts if they are recent college graduates and associates if they are recent MBA graduates.) Some of the most common transactions that investment bankers work on are initial public offerings (IPOs) and company mergers and acquisitions. Typically, analysts and associates work between 80 and 100 hours per week preparing presentations and financial models for banking clients.

Positions in research

Other popular sell-side positions for young financial professionals can be found in the research department. Research professionals analyze company and industry fundamentals, predict earnings and cash flows, determine appropriate valuations, and recommend investments to buy-side clients. Typically, recent graduates hired out of college work as assistants to senior industry research analysts. Individuals hired from business schools generally start as research associates working directly with the lead industry analyst.

Sell-side research assistants spend the majority of their day gathering industry data, populating investment models and preparing the foundations of company and industry reports.

Sell-side research associates build investment models, assist in generating investment recommendations, write company and industry reports and help to communicate recommendations to buy-side clients.

On the surface, the roles of buy-side and sell-side analysts sound remarkably similar. However, the day-to-day job is quite different. Sell-side analysts not only generate investment recommendations, they also need to market their ideas. This involves publishing elaborate and lengthy investment reports and meeting with their buy-side clients. In contrast, the buy-side analyst focuses entirely on investment analysis. The buy-side analyst also works directly with portfolio managers at the same firm, making it easier to focus on the relevant components of the analysis. The sell-side analyst is writing not for a specific team of professionals, but for the buy-side industry as a whole.

Despite these differences in responsibilities, professionals in buy-side and sell-side research analyst positions develop similar skill sets. In fact, sell-side research and investment banking positions are the most popular training grounds for finance professionals who eventually switch to the buy-side.

How do the buy-side and sell-side interact?

Sell-side firms earn a trading fee every time a security (such as a bond or a stock) is bought or sold in a buy-side firm's portfolio. Because portfolio trades can generate sizeable commissions, sell-side firms (investment banks) have quite an incentive to develop relationships with the asset managers. Through institutional salespeople, investment banks provide asset managers with services such as analyst recommendations and access to firm-sponsored IPOs and debt offerings. Additionally, the traders and salespeople who want asset managers' business will often present them with gifts such as expensive dinners and tickets to sporting events. An investment management professional in New York says, "I have been to a Yankees games, a Knicks game, the U.S. Open, a rock concert, and eaten at over a dozen of the city's finest expensive restaurants. It's good to be the client." At the same time, another insider from a major asset management remarks, "It's important to be somewhat conservative. No firm wants to have it known that their guys have a lavish lifestyle and are out partying all night long; it might make it hard to convince the Carpenter's Union that you will do the best job possible managing their money."

For a detailed look at the career paths and hiring process for investment banking, sales & trading, and research professionals, get the best-selling Vault Career Guide to Investment Banking. Also consult our expert investment banking career advice and message boards at the Vault web site.

Go to the Vault Finance Career Channel at http://finance.vault.com

Compensation

In general, compensation in asset management is a combination of base salary and bonus. As you move up in the organization to senior portfolio manager or senior sales and marketing official, for example, your pay becomes more heavily weighted toward bonuses. Senior portfolio manager pay is somewhat contingent upon relative investment fund performance, size of the fund managed, new assets invested in the fund and overall firm performance. Senior sales and marketing compensation is weighted toward new account generation and the level of attrition by existing accounts.

Mid-level investment staff are paid both a salary and bonus. Bonuses are based less on specific investment results (given that these people have less impact on the actual performance). Instead, performance reviews are based on individual contributions, value added to the team and overall firm results. The split between salary and bonus is more heavily weighted to salary than at the senior levels.

Entry-level assistants are also compensated with salary and bonus, but the majority is weighted toward salary. Performance-based bonuses are a function of overall firm and division results as well as contributions made in their role. The spread between high and low bonuses to entry-level positions is much narrower than at the mid and senior levels of the organization.

Recommended Reading

Preparing for a career in investment management requires the same research as any other field. So other than this Vault Career Guide and the Vault web site, what are some resources for the future money manager?

There are many textbooks that teach you various technical skills or outline the author's investment philosophy and techniques. These types of books are easily found in any library or bookstore. Harder to find are books that tell you about what the actual experience of working in this business is like. Unfortunately, there are no equivalents to the numerous books describing authors' experiences in investment banking (John Rolfe and Peter Troob's *Monkey Business*, Michael Lewis' *Liar's Poker* and Frank Partnoy's *F.I.A.S.C.O.*). Part of the reason for this is that most buy-siders are in the business permanently – nobody is going to write an account of how they misspent their days at Fidelity or Putnam when they're still working in the business (and may well have gotten their current position on the strength of their experience at Fidelity or Putnam).

That said, below are some books that will give you a good idea of the actual life and career investment managers lead.

Primers

• Gremillion, Lee, *A Purely American Invention: The U.S. Open-End Mutual Fund Industry* (National Investment Company Service Association, 2000.)

Gremillion is a partner in PricewaterhouseCoopers Investment Management consulting group. He was previously a professor at Indiana University and Boston University. Like Pozen's *Mutual Fund Business*, this book provides the basic info on the business.

• Pozen, Robert and Crane, Sandra, *The Mutual Fund Business* (MIT Press, 1998.)

Robert Pozen is the former president of Fidelity Management and Research. This book is a collection of essays and statistics that provide the fundamentals of the business. Not exactly a page-turner, but a valuable primer nonetheless.

Autobiographies and histories

- Dreyfus, Jack, *The Lion of Wall Street: The Two Lives of Jack Dreyfus* (Regnery, 1996.)

Jack Dreyfus founded the firm that bears his name and was a pioneer in the mutual fund industry. In this amusing autobiography, Dreyfus recounts his professional life. Due to an onset of clinical depression, Dreyfus began a lifelong crusade to encourage the FDA to approve the drug Dilantin, the retelling of which makes up the second half of the book.

- Ellis, Charles and Vertin, James, *Wall Street People: True Stories of Today's Masters and Moguls* (John Wiley & Sons, 2001.)

Ellis and Vertin both have had an inestimable impact on modern portfolio management. This book has interviews with some of the most prominent figures in modern investing: Jim Rogers, George Soros, Warren Buffett and Larry Tisch are just a few of the people they talk to here.

- Fisher, Phil A, *Common Stocks and Uncommon Profits* (John Wiley & Sons, 1996.)

Phil Fisher is one of the greatest growth investors in history. This book leads you through the development of his philosophy and firm, Fisher & Company, as well as illustrating some major investment decisions he made.

- Henriques, Diana, *Fidelity's World: The Secret Life and Public Power of the Mutual Fund Giant* (Touchstone, 1997.)

Henriques discusses the history, business practices and inner life of the industry leader.

- Lowenstein, Roger, *When Genius Failed: The Rise and Fall of Long-Term Capital Management* (Random House, 2000.)

Lowenstein, a *Wall Street Journal* reporter, describes the founding and eventual crash of the only hedge fund ever to have several Nobel Prize winners on staff. A fascinating read.

- Neuberger, Roy, *So Far, So Good: The First 94 Years* (John Wiley & Sons, 2000.)

Roy Neuberger has been on the Street since 1929 and is a co-founder of Boston-based Neuberger & Berman. His autobiography tells of his professional and personal life, in addition to his extensive collection of American modernist paintings.

- Niederhoffer, Victor, *Education of a Speculator* (John Wiley & Sons, 1998.)

Niederhoffer runs a hedge fund whose performance has been quite volatile. This book is a charming (though quite eccentric) autobiography. Niederhoffer, by the way, collects rare books.

- Sosnoff, Martin, *Silent Investor, Silent Loser* (Richardson, Steirman & Black, 1987)

Sosnoff is a co-founder of Atlanta / Sosnoff Capital and one of the best thinkers on the Street. In addition to his professional life, Sosnoff describes, in-depth, some of the actual investment decisions he has made in the past. Sosnoff is also a prominent collector of American modernist paintings.

Newspapers, magazines and journals

- *Barron's*
- *Financial Analyst Journal*
- *Institutional Investor*
- *Journal of Portfolio Management*
- *Pensions and Investments*
- *The Wall Street Journal*

Reference books

- *Nelson's Directory of Investment Managers*
- *Nelson's Directory of Investment Research*

The Clients of Asset Managers

As you can see from our initial discussion, the structure of the asset management industry can seem a bit complicated. Don't worry – over the next two chapters, we will explain how buy-side firms operate so you can easily understand how they fit together. Specifically, we'll discuss:

1) The clients investment management firms serve

2) The investment styles used by the firms

Armed with this knowledge, you'll be ready to organize your career search in a targeted and effective manner.

Different types of clients

Typically, asset management firms are categorized according to the kind of clients they serve. Clients generally fall into one of three categories: 1) mutual funds, 2) institutional investors, or 3) high net worth. Some firms specialize in one of the three components, but most participate in all three. Asset management firms usually assemble these three areas as distinct and separate divisions within the company.

It is critical that you understand the differences between these client types; job descriptions vary depending on the type. For instance, a portfolio manager for high-net-worth individuals has an inherently different focus than one representing institutional clients. A marketing professional working for a mutual fund has a vastly different job than one handling pensions for an investment management firm. Later in this Guide, we will discuss how different positions in the industry differ across the main organizing features of the industry (client types and investment style).

For now, we'll begin our discussion of the industry by examining different client types.

Mutual Funds

Mutual funds are investment vehicles for individual investors who are typically below the status of high net worth (we will discuss individual high net worth investing later in this chapter). Mutual funds are also sometimes known as the retail division of asset management firms.

Mutual funds are structured so that each investor owns a share of the fund – investors do not maintain separate portfolios, but rather pool their money together. Their broad appeal can generally be attributed to the ease of investing through them and the relatively small contribution needed to diversify investments. Investment gains from mutual funds are taxable unless the investment is through an employee 401(k) plan or an Individual Retirement Account (IRA). (If you take some money you've saved and invest in a mutual fund, you'll have to pay capital gains taxes on your earnings.)

In the past 10 years, mutual funds have become an increasingly integral part of the asset management industry. They generally constitute a large portion of a firm's assets under management (AUMs) and ultimate profitability.

There are three ways that mutual funds are sold to the individuals that invest in them: 1) through third-party brokers or "fund supermarkets"; 2) direct to customer; and 3) though company 401(k) plans. The size and breadth of the asset management company typically dictates whether one, two, or all three of the methods are used.

Third-party brokers and "fund supermarkets"

Over the past five years, an increasingly popular distribution platform for mutual funds has been to sell them through brokerage firms or "fund supermarkets." By selling through these channels, asset management companies can leverage the huge access to clients that the brokers maintain. In a classic broker relationship, a company with a sales force partners with several investment management firms to offer their investment products. Then, for instance, Merrill Lynch and Morgan Stanley not only sell their own mutual funds, but offer their clients access to mutual funds from Vanguard, Putnam and AIM as well. This additional access to multiple mutual fund products helps the brokers win business; brokers earn a commission from the asset management companies they recommend. Brokers develop relationships with individual investors not only by executing trades, but also by dispensing advice and research.

Fund supermarkets, such as Charles Schwab, became increasingly popular in the late 1990s. These firms are set up similarly to brokerage houses, but the supermarkets carry virtually every major asset management firm's products, don't expend as much energy on providing advice and other relationship-building activities and take lower commissions. The rise of the fund supermarkets has forced conventional brokerage firms to open up their offerings to include more than a few select partners. It has also influenced the way mutual funds market themselves. Previously, funds marketed to brokers and expected them to push their products to individual investors. Now, mutual fund companies increasingly must appeal directly to investors themselves (which is why you see so much advertising for companies like Fidelity and Vanguard).

Direct to customer

Through an internal sales force, asset management companies offer clients access to the firm's entire suite of mutual funds. This type of sales force is very expensive to maintain, but some companies, such as Fidelity and T. Rowe Price, have been extremely successful with this method. Prior to the rise of brokers and fund supermarkets, direct to customer was the primary vehicle for investment in many mutual funds – if you wanted a Fidelity fund, you had to open an account with Fidelity.

401(k) plans

An increasingly popular sales channel for mutual funds is the 401(k) retirement plan. Under 401(k) plans, employees can set aside pre-tax money for their retirements. Employers hire asset management firms to facilitate all aspects of their employees' 401(k) accounts, including the mutual fund options offered. By capturing the management of these 401(k) assets, the firms dramatically increase the sale and exposure of their mutual fund products. In fact, many asset management companies have developed separate divisions that manage the 401(k) programs for companies of all sizes.

Below is a list of the firms with the largest amount of mutual fund assets under management. We have also included the 10 largest mutual funds and the assets that are invested in each. As we noted earlier, consolidation and global competition has created a small group of very large players in the mutual fund marketplace.

Top 10 Managers of Mutual Fund Assets	AUM's as of 12/31/01 ($ millions)
Fidelity Investments	$798,627
Vanguard Group	$580,560
Capital Research	$367,056
Morgan Stanley	$278,357
Merrill Lynch	$220,000
Putnam Investments	$218,688
Citigroup Asset Management	$209,023
UBS Global Asset Management	$207,238
Franklin Templeton	$197,445
Wellington	$185,478

Source: Pensions & Investments, May 2002

10 Largest Mutual Funds	AUM's as of 4/5/02 ($ millions)
Fidelity Magellan	$75,380
Vanguard 500 Index	$72,290
American Funds – America A	$54,010
American Funds – Washington Mutual	$48,920
American Funds – Growth Fund	$36,080
PIMCO Total Return	$35,360
Fidelity Growth and Income	$33,500
Fidelity Contrafund	$31,710
American Funds – New Perspective	$27,150
American Funds – Euro Pacific Growth	$26,540

Source: The Wall Street Journal

Institutional Investors

Institutional investors are very different from their mutual fund brethren. These clients represent large pools of assets for government pension funds, corporate pension funds, endowments and foundations. Institutional investors are also referred to in the industry as "sophisticated investors" and are usually represented by corporate treasurers, CFOs and pension boards.

More conservative

Given their fiduciary responsibility to the people whose retirement assets they manage, institutional clients are usually more conservative and diversified than mutual funds.

Unlike investors in mutual funds, institutional clients have separately managed portfolios that, at a minimum, exceed $10 million. Also unlike mutual funds, they are all exempt from capital gains and investment income.

Below is a list of the largest institutional asset managers. As you can see, a few are also listed as leaders on the mutual fund chart. But for the most part, these institutional managers are different firms; as mentioned previously, different factors lead to success for different investment clients (we highlight the nuances later in this chapter).

Top 10 Firms Ranked by Worldwide Institutional Assets Under Management	AUM's as of 12/31/01 ($ millions)
State Street Global	$75,380
Barclay's Global	$72,290
Fidelity Investments	$54,010
Deutsche Asset Management	$48,920
JP Morgan Fleming	$36,080
AIG Global	$35,360
Vanguard Group	$33,500
Merrill Lynch	$31,710
TIAA-CREF	$27,150
Alliance Capital	$26,540

Source: Pension and Investments, May 2002

Institutional clients hold enormous sums of capital that they must allocate in order to meet the needs of the beneficiaries of the retirement assets. Consequently, the representatives hire multiple institutional asset managers to manage across the full range of investment styles (these styles, such as growth stocks and value stocks, will be detailed in the next chapter).

Below is a list of the largest pension funds in the U.S. Funds like CalPERS and General Motors hold well over $100 billion for their retirees. These funds have relationships with many different asset managers and have separate portfolios that cut across every asset class and investment style imaginable. Clearly, developing relationships with these large clients can be highly profitable for the asset management firms.

10 Largest Pension Funds in the U.S.	Assets as of 12/31/00 ($ millions)
CalPERS – California Public Employees	$171,542
New York State Common	$124,973
California State Teachers	$111,552
Florida State Board	$106,328
General Motors	$105,800
Federal Retirement Thrift	$100,191
New York State Teachers	$90,093
General Electric	$88,490
Texas Teachers	$87,150
New Jersey Division	$82,052

Source: Pension & Investments, December 24, 2001

Method of selection

Given the high level of responsibility associated with managing portfolios of these sizes, pension funds utilize a rigorous process of selecting asset managers. In turn, asset management companies have built considerable marketing and sales departments to cater to institutional clients. The selection process typically works as follows:

- An institution, say a pension fund, issues a request for proposal (an RFP), announcing that it is searching for new investment managers in a particular style or asset class.

- Asset management companies respond to the RFP, elaborating on their products, services and credentials.

- Investment consultants are hired by the pension fund to help sort through the RFPs and narrow the list of firms to three to five finalists.

- The finalists meet in person with the pension fund's representatives and further due diligence is performed before the winner is selected.

Due to the sophistication of this process, there are many interesting professional jobs in the institutional sales, marketing and relationship management functions. If you are interested in the investment business, but don't necessarily want to participate in analyzing and selecting portfolio investments, these are career paths that you may wish to pursue (we discuss this in greater detail in later sections).

In the mutual fund world, individuals tend to select funds based on recent performance records and brand recognition. Institutions tend to select asset managers under a much more stringent and analytical process. Specifically, they use the following criteria: 1) superior performance record relative to the firm's peer group, 2) length of investment track record, 3) continuity of the existing core investment team, and 4) consistency in adhering to a specific investment style and discipline.

High Net Worth

High-net-worth individuals represent the smallest but fastest growing client type. Individual wealth creation and financial sophistication over the past decade has driven asset managers to focus heavily in this area. Despite the success of many large asset management firms in the area, the firms that specialize in high net worth clients, such as Bessemer Trust and Pell Rudman, remain the leaders in this business.

What is high net?

What is a high-net-worth investor? Definitions differ, but a good rule of thumb is an individual with minimum asset portfolios of $5 to $10 million. These investors are typically taxable (like mutual funds, but unlike institutional investors), but their portfolio accounts are managed separately (unlike mutual funds, but like institutions).

High-net-worth investors also require high levels of client service (read: hand-holding). Those considering entering this side of the market should be prepared to be as interested in client relationship management as in portfolio management, although the full force of client relations is borne not by a portfolio manager but a sell-side salesperson in a firm's Private Client Services (PCS) division. Says one investment manager about PCS sales, "If [clients] tell them they're out of paper towels, they'll probably go to their houses and bring them [paper towels]." (For more information about lucrative PCS career opportunities, see the *Vault Career Guide to Investment Banking*.)

In reality, there are two classes of high-net-worth clients: those in the $2 million and above range, and those in the $500,000 to $2 million range. Those with $2 million and above to invest receive customized and separately managed portfolios, while those in the $500,000 to $2 million arena do not. This second class does receive much more personal attention from their PCS salesperson than they would from a traditional retail broker. But, unlike the $2 million and above range people, this second group's portfolio management is derived from cookie cutter products and strategies. Still, this service is performed by a portfolio manager devoted to high-net-worth clients, and assets aren't actually lumped into a large fund as they would be in a mutual fund.

High-net-worth investors also often use the institutions that manage their assets for other financial services, such as estate planning or tax work.

Clients and consultants

An investment management firm's relationship management sales force typically sells high-net-worth services in one of two ways: either directly to wealthy individuals, or to third parties called investment consultants who work for wealthy individuals. The first method is fairly straightforward. An investment manager's sales force, the PCS unit, pitches services directly to the individuals with the money. In the second method, a firm's internal sales force does not directly pitch those with the money, but rather pitches representatives, often called investment consultants, of high-net-worth clients. In general, investment consultants play a much smaller role in the high-net-worth area than the institutional side; only extremely wealthy individuals will enlist investment consultant firms to help them decide which investment manager to go with.

The Investment Consultant

Not to be confused with retail brokers, investment consultants are third-party firms enlisted by institutional investors, and to a lesser extent by high-net-worth individuals, to aid in the following: devising appropriate asset allocations, selecting investment managers to fulfill these allocations, and monitoring the chosen investment managers' services. An investment consultant might be hired by a client to assist in one or all of these functions depending on certain variables, such as the client's size and internal resources.

As an example of the part that investment consultants play in the investment management game, let's say GM's pension fund is looking to invest $50 million in a certain security sector (say, large cap value equities). GM hires Wilshire Associates, an investment consulting firm, to help it find a large cap value manager. Wilshire will go out and search for the best managers in the sector and, one month later, will come back to GM with three recommendations. GM will review the three firms and then pick one. After GM makes its decision and the $50 million is handed over to the chosen investment manger, Wilshire might also monitor that manager's investment decisions.

True intermediaries, investment consultants have become increasingly important in the past 10 years as a result of a rise in the number of different investment product offerings.

Some of the biggest names in investment consulting:

- Frank Russell Company
- Wilshire Associates
- Mercer Investment Consulting
- Watson Wyatt Worldwide
- Callan Associates
- Barra RogersCasey
- Evaluation Associates
- Capital Resource Advisors
- Ennis, Knupp & Associates
- R.V. Kuhns & Associates
- Hewitt Investment Group
- The Marco Consulting Alliance
- DeMarche Associates

Competition on the Street – and beyond – is heating up. With the finance job market tightening, you need to be your best.

We know the finance industry. And we've got experts that know the finance environment standing by to review your resume and give you the boost you need to snare the financial position you deserve.

Finance Resume Writing and Resume Reviews

- Have your resume reviewed by a practicing finance professional.

- For resume writing, start with an e-mailed history and 1- to 2-hour phone discussion. Our experts will write a first draft, and deliver a final draft after feedback and discussion.

- For resume reviews, get an in-depth, detailed critique and rewrite within TWO BUSINESS DAYS.

Finance Career Coaching

Have a pressing finance career situation you need Vault's expert advice with? We've got experts who can help.

- Trying to get into investment banking from business school or other careers?

- Switching from one finance sector to another – for example, from commercial banking to investment banking?

- Trying to figure out the cultural fit of the finance firm you should work for?

For more information go to http://finance.vault.com

VAULT
> the insider career network™

Investment Styles

CHAPTER 4

The three types of investment styles

Investment style refers to the way a portfolio is managed. These styles are typically classified in one of three ways:

1) The type of security (i.e., stocks vs. bonds)

2) The risk characteristics of the investments (i.e., growth vs. value stocks, or U.S. Treasury vs. "junk" bonds)

3) The manner in which the portfolio is constructed (i.e., active vs. passive funds)

It is important to note that each of these styles is relevant to all of the client types covered in the previous chapter (mutual fund, institutional and high-net-worth investing).

The drive for diversification

The investment industry's maturation over the last 20 years has been led by the power of portfolio theory and investors' desire for diversification of investments. During this period, investors have grown more sophisticated, and have increasingly looked for multiple investment styles to diversify their wealth.

Typically, investors (whether they be individual or institutional) allocate various portions of their assets to different investment styles. If you think of the overall wealth of an individual or institution as a pie, you can think of each slice as investing in a different portfolio of securities – this is what's called diversification. The style of a portfolio, such as a mutual fund, is clearly indicated through its name and marketing materials so investors know what to expect from it. Adherence to the styles marketed is more heavily scrutinized by institutions and pension funds than by mutual fund customers. Institutional investors monitor their funds every day to make sure that the asset manager is investing in the way they said they would.

In the following sections, we will describe each investment style classification in detail.

Type of Security

Type of security is the most straightforward category of investment style. Investment portfolios invest in either equity or debt.

Stocks

Equity portfolios invest in the stock of public companies. This means that the portfolios are purchasing a share of the company – they are actually becoming owners of the company and, as a result, directly benefit if the company performs well. Equity investors may reap these benefits in the form of dividends (the distribution of profits to shareholders), or simply through an increase in share price.

Bonds

Fixed income portfolios invest in bonds, a different type of security than stocks. Bonds can be thought of as loans issued by organizations like companies or municipalities. (In fact, bonds are often referred to simply as "debt.") Like loans, bonds have a fixed term of existence, and pay a fixed rate of return. For example, a company may issue a 5-year bond that pays a 7 percent annual return. This company is then under a contractual obligation to pay this interest amount to bondholders, as well as return the original amount at the end of the term. While bondholders aren't "owners" of the bond issuer in the same way that equity shareholders are, they maintain a claim on its assets as creditors. If a company cannot pay its bond obligations, bondholders may take control of its assets (in the same way that a bank can repossess your car if you don't make your payments).

Although bonds have fixed rates of return, their actual prices fluctuate in the securities market just like stock prices do. (Just like there is a stock market where investors buy and sell stocks, there is a bond market where investors buy and sell bonds.) In the case of bonds, investors are willing to pay more or less for debt depending on how likely they think it is that the bond issuer will be able to pay its obligations.

Risk Characteristics of Investments

Types of stocks and their risk profiles

Most equity portfolios are classified in two ways:

1) By size, or market capitalization, of the companies whose stocks are invested in by the portfolios.

2) By risk profile of the stocks, which is often related to market capitalization but is not directly correlated.

Market capitalization of investments

The market capitalization (also known as "market cap") of a company refers to the company's total value according to the stock market. It is simply the product of the company's current stock price and the number of shares outstanding. For example, a company with a stock price of $10 and 10 million outstanding shares has a market cap of $100 million.

Companies (and their stocks) are usually categorized as small-, mid- or large-capitalization. Most equity portfolios focus on one type, but some invest across market capitalization.

While definitions vary, small-capitalization typically means any company less than $300 million, mid-capitalization constitutes $300 million to $1.5 billion, and large-capitalization is the label for firms in excess of $1.5 billion. As would be expected, large-capitalization stocks primarily constitute well-established companies with long standing track records. While this is generally true, the tremendous growth of new technology companies over the past decade has propelled many fledgling companies into the ranks of large-capitalization. For instance, Microsoft has a market-capitalization in the hundreds of billions of dollars and is one of the largest companies in the world. In the same way, small and medium capitalization stocks not only include new or under-recognized companies, but also sometimes include established firms that have struggled recently and have seen their market caps fall.

Risk profiles: "value" vs. "growth" investing

Generally, equity portfolios are defined as investing in either "value" or "growth" – terms that attempt to express expected rates of return and risk. There are many ways that investors define these styles, but most explanations center on valuation. Value stocks can be characterized as relatively well-established, high dividend-paying companies with low price-to-earnings and price-to-book ratios. Essentially, they are "diamonds in the rough" that typically have undervalued assets and earnings potential. Classic value stocks include oil companies like ExxonMobil and banks such as Bank of America or J.P. Morgan Chase.

Growth stocks are industry leaders that investors believe will continue to prosper and exceed expectations. These companies have above average revenue and earnings growth and their stocks trade at high price to earnings and price to book ratios. Technology and telecommunications companies such as Microsoft and Cisco are good examples of traditional growth stocks.

Many variations of growth and value portfolios exist in the marketplace today. For instance, "aggressive growth" portfolios invest in companies that are growing rapidly through innovation or new industry developments. These investments are relatively speculative and offer higher returns with higher risk. Many biotechnology companies and new Internet stocks in the late 1990s would have been classified as aggressive growth. Another classification is a "core stock" portfolio, which is a middle ground that blends investment in both growth and value stocks.

Putting it together

As you can imagine, there are many combinations of size and style variations and equally as many portfolios and investment products. For example, you have your choice of investing in small-cap growth stock portfolios, mid-cap value stock portfolios or large-cap core stock portfolios. (Or you can invest in small-cap value stock portfolios, mid-cap growth stock portfolios, and so on.)

In general, the smaller the company (small-cap stocks), the riskier its stock is considered.

This is because large companies are usually older and better established: it's easier to make predictions of large-cap stocks because they have more historical financial data from which analysts can base predictions. Growth stocks are also considered riskier, as investments in those stocks are bets on continued rapid growth (reflected in the high price-to-earnings ratio of these stocks).

These risk factors are not always predictive, of course. Enron and WorldCom, for example, were both large-cap stocks that turned out to be very risky. The chart on page 41 details risk characteristics for these various combinations.

Types of bonds and their risk profiles

Just like stock portfolios, fixed income (bond) portfolios vary in their focus. The most common way to classify them is as follows

1) Government bonds

2) Investment-grade corporate bonds

3) High-yield corporate bonds

4) Municipal bonds

Government bond portfolios invest in the debt issues from the U.S. Treasury or other federal agencies. These investments tend to have low risk and low returns because of the financial stability of the U.S. government.

Investment-grade corporate bond portfolios invest in the debt issued by companies with high credit standings. These credit ratings are issued by rating companies like Moody's and Standard & Poor's. They rate debt based on the likelihood that a company will meet the interest obligations of the debt. Moody's, for example, rates investment grade debt from Aaa (the highest quality; most likely to meet interest payments) to Baa (lower quality; less likely). The returns and risks of these investments vary along this rating spectrum. Many corporate bond portfolios invest in company debt that ranges the entire continuum of high-grade debt.

In contrast to investment grade debt, **high-yield corporate debt**, also called "junk bonds," is the debt issued by smaller, unproven or high-risk companies. Consequently, the risk and expected rates of return are higher. (Junk, or high-yield, is defined as a bond with a Standard & Poor's rating below BBB and/or a Moody's rating below Baa.)

Finally, **municipal bond portfolios** invest in the debt issued by local governments and agencies, such as public school systems or state-funded projects. The favorable tax treatment on these types of investments makes them a favorite of tax-sensitive investors.

Investment managers also manage bond portfolios that mix together the different types of bonds. Indeed, hybrids of all kinds exist. Typically, though, if you have a lot of money, a better way to diversify is to invest in a fund made up of one type of bond. If, for example, you've got $100 million to invest, you're likely to give $10 million to the best municipal bond fund manager, $10 million to the best corporate bond fund manager, etc., rather than invest all $100 million in a hybrid.

Investment decisions

Just as with equity portfolios, there are a myriad of fixed income portfolio types. While the ratings issued by agencies like Moody's and Standard & Poor's provide investment managers with a guideline and starting point for determining the risk of a bond, managers also form independent opinions on risk, and make investment decisions based on whether they feel they have a good chance of receiving the promised payments.

The easiest way to see this is to consider a junk bond. When a company that many analysts think is at risk of performing poorly issues bonds, it must promise a high rate of return because of its credit rating. An individual asset manager, however, through analysis of the company and its industry, may believe that the company has a good chance of performing well. The manager would likely then decide that the company's debt is a good investment.

Portfolio Construction

All portfolios, whether they are stock or bond portfolios, are compared to benchmarks to gauge their performance; indices or peer group statistics are used to monitor the success of each fund. Standard indices for equity portfolios include the S&P 500, Wilshire 5000, Russell 2000 and the S&P Value and Growth. For bonds, popular benchmarks include the Lehman Government/Corporate Bond Index and the J.P. Morgan Emerging Market Bond Index. These indices are composed of representative stocks or bonds. They function as a general barometer of the performance of the particular portion of the market they are designed to measure.

As composites, the indices can be thought of as similar to polls: a polling firm that seeks to understand what a certain population thinks about a certain issue will ask representatives of that cross-section of the population. Similarly, a stock or bond benchmark that seeks to measure a certain portion of the market will simply compile the values of representative stocks or bonds.

Portfolio construction refers to the manner in which securities are selected and then weighted in the overall mix of the portfolio with respect to these indices. Portfolio construction is a fairly recent phenomenon, and has been driven by the advent of modern portfolio theory.

Passive investors or index funds

Portfolios that are constructed to mimic the composition of various benchmarks are referred to as index funds. Investors in index funds are classified as passive investors, and investment managers who manage index funds are often called "indexers." These funds are continually tinkered with to ensure that they match the performance of the index. For equities, the S&P 500 is the benchmark that is most commonly indexed.

Active investors

Portfolios that are constructed by consciously selecting securities without reference to the index are referred to as active portfolios. Active portfolios adhere to their own investment discipline, and investment managers actually invest in what they think are the best stocks or bonds. They are then compared, for performance purposes only, to the pre-selected index that best represents their style. For instance, many large-capitalization active value portfolios are compared to either the S&P 500 Value index or the Russell

1000 Value index. (It is important to note that while active portfolios are still compared to indices, they are not designed specifically to mimic the indices.)

Alternative methods

Variations of active and passive portfolios are present throughout the marketplace. There are enhanced index funds that closely examine the benchmark before making an investment. These portfolios mimic the overall characteristics of the benchmark and make small bets that differentiate the portfolio from its index.

Asset management firms also organize and market funds in categories that we have not discussed. One of the most common alternative methods used is sector investing. This is a method of investing that utilizes portfolios composed of companies in a specific industry. Common sector portfolios include technology, health care, biotechnology and financial services. For example, many firms construct funds based on geographic regions. Thus, there are U.S. growth stock funds or emerging market fixed income funds. Firms also even market funds based on politics (e.g., environment-friendly funds).

Summary of Investment Styles

Ultimately, the various investment styles discussed above translate into various investment products. The chart below summarizes the resulting investment products that are offered by most diversified asset managers. Mutual fund, institutional and high-net-worth investors select the appropriate product that best matches their risk and diversification needs.

Overview of Products – Based on Investment Styles

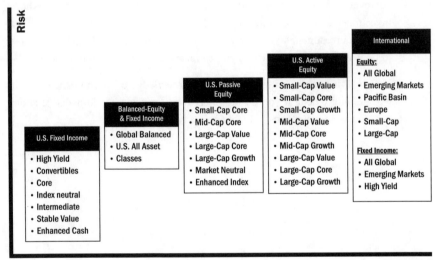

How Is This Relevant to My Job Search?

If you are beginning your job search in the investment management industry, you need to begin thinking about what investment styles strike you as most interesting. While many of the styles overlap, and being overly specific might limit you, understanding the difference can help in targeting companies you want to work for. For instance, Vanguard is known mainly for its passive index investment style. If you are more interested in investing in actively managed bond portfolios, then Vanguard probably isn't your best bet, and you should try PIMCO Advisors instead.

Don't be concerned that your choice of employer will pigeonhole you, however. While you should try to find a position with a firm whose investment style most interests you, you can always switch gears into a different investment style after you have some experience. Initially, it is best to be in an environment where you can learn about investing in general.

However, it is always important to have knowledge of these nuances. This will definitely benefit you during interviews – passion and knowledge about the industry always wins valuable points with recruiters.

ON THE JOB

Chapter 5: Portfolio Management

Chapter 6: Investment Research

Chapter 7: Marketing/Sales

Chapter 8: Days in the Life

Increase your T/NJ Ratio
(Time to New Job)

Use the Internet's most targeted

job search tools for finance

professionals.

Vault Finance Job Board

The most comprehensive and convenient job board for finance
professionals. Target your search by area of finance, function,
and experience level, and find the job openings that you want.
No surfing required.

VaultMatch Resume Database

Vault takes match-making to the next level: post your resume
and customize your search by area of finance, experience and
more. We'll match job listings with your interests and criteria
and e-mail them directly to your inbox.

Portfolio Management

CHAPTER 5

The Three Segments

As we discussed in Chapter 2, asset management firms are organized into three segments: portfolio management, investment research and marketing/sales. Below is a diagram that explains this structure. As you can see from the dotted lines, portfolio management as well as marketing and sales directly serve the client (whether they be individuals, institutions or high-net-worth investors). Alternatively, investment research has a dotted line to portfolio management, indicating its support of the investment process (analysts have no direct client exposure). In the following sections, we will describe the three segments and the jobs associated with each.

Professional Positions in Asset Management

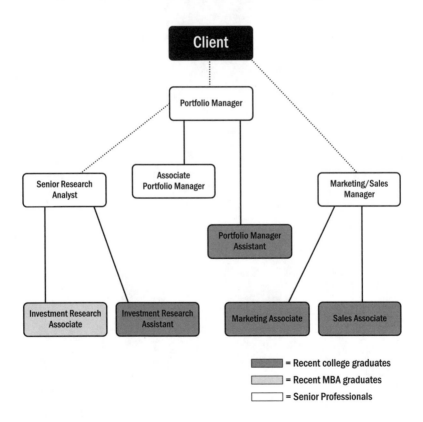

Portfolio Management

The portfolio management segment of the firm makes the ultimate investment decision; it's the department that "pulls the trigger." There are three jobs that typically fall under this component of the firm: portfolio managers, associate portfolio managers and portfolio manager assistants. Recent college graduates often fill portfolio assistant positions, while individuals with many years of investment experience hold associate and senior portfolio manager assignments. MBAs are not hired as portfolio managers right out of business school unless they have a ton of experience. Typically, MBAs who wish to pursue a career in portfolio management join investment management firms in their investment research divisions. After two years in research, MBAs will then have a choice: either stay in research or leverage their research experience to move into an associate portfolio manager position.

Senior Portfolio Manager

Portfolio managers are responsible for establishing an investment strategy, selecting appropriate investments and allocating each investment properly. All day long, portfolio managers are presented with investment ideas from internal buy-side analysts and sell-side analysts from investment banks. It is their job to sift through the relevant information and use their judgment to buy and sell securities. Throughout each day, they read reports, talk to company managers and monitor industry and economic trends looking for the right company and time to invest the portfolio's capital.

The selection of investments must adhere to the style of the portfolio. For instance, a large-capitalization growth manager might be screening for only companies that have a market-capitalization in excess of $3 billion and earnings growth characteristics that exceed its industry. Therefore, the portfolio manager would not even consider a $500 million utility stock with a 6 percent dividend yield.

Once investment opportunities are recognized, portfolio managers must decide what percentage of their portfolio to allocate to the respective security. This decision is based on the mandate of the portfolio – active or passive – and the risk expectation of the overall portfolio. For example, riskier portfolios invest in a small number of securities and take large "bets." The popular Janus Twenty fund invests in only 20 liquid large-capitalization companies. Alternatively, diversified portfolios may invest in over 100 securities to spread the risk of any one holding.

Portfolio managers also spend time meeting with their clients to review investment strategy and performance results. While marketing and sales professionals lead this process, portfolio managers are often an integral part of client discussions. In the mutual fund world, portfolio managers don't spend time talking to individual customers, but they are often called on to present at sales conferences and at product road shows. However, institutional and high-net-worth portfolio managers have fewer clients, and they only meet with them one to two times a year.

Portfolio managers are the most seasoned investment professionals in the firm. Typically, people with at least 7 to 10 years of investment experience occupy these positions, and most have either an MBA or a CFA designation.

Associate Portfolio Manager

The associate portfolio manager position requires an MBA, CFA or considerable investment experience. Typically, the job is filled by successful research analysts who have at least 3 to 5 years of post-MBA experience. The job itself is very similar to that of the senior portfolio manager with one main exception: associates interact less with clients than senior managers do. Associate portfolio managers are usually assigned smaller, less sophisticated portfolios to manage or serve as lieutenants on large, complicated portfolios.

The role of the associate portfolio manager differs depending on which segment of the market is being served – mutual fund, institutional or high-net-worth. For instance, associate portfolio managers at many mutual fund firms will either act as the lead investor on a sector fund or as second-in-command on a large diversified fund. Depending on the firm, an associate could also act as a lead on a sector fund and a second-in-command on a diversified fund at the same time. Alternatively, on the institutional side, associate portfolio managers typically apprentice with seasoned portfolio managers on the largest and most complicated portfolios. After they have succeeded in that role, the firm will assign them smaller institutional accounts to manage on their own.

Successful associate portfolio managers will usually be promoted to senior portfolio managers within 2 to 5 years.

Associate Portfolio Manager

Uppers	Downers
• Great spot to showcase your investment talent • Clearest path to running the big-time portfolios • Autonomy and creative independence	• Always being graded on your investment decisions • Competitive, high level of scrutiny • Limited client interaction • High degree of focus, smaller accounts or sector funds

Portfolio Manager Assistant

In general, portfolio manager assistants screen for potential investments, monitor portfolio characteristics, and assist in client relations. Recent college graduates typically will spend 2 to 4 years in this role before returning to business school or migrating to a role in the investment research department.

This position varies among the firms in the industry, and the role itself differs depending on which segment of the firm you work in – mutual fund, institutional or high-net-worth. For instance, high-net-worth portfolio assistants spend more time working with clients, while institutional assistants spend more time monitoring and analyzing portfolios. Regardless, the general assignment focuses on supporting the portfolio manager.

Portfolio manager assistants are often instrumental in the process of screening for potential investments. Using the general strategy of the investment product – such as market-capitalization, earnings growth, valuation multiples or industry – the assistant screens all available stocks in the market (about 10,000) to identify the smaller list that meets the portfolio's criteria. The screened list for an active portfolio varies, but typically ranges between 100 and 300 securities. Portfolio manager assistants then gather additional research for the portfolio manager to begin the process of fundamentally analyzing the potential investment.

Once investments are made, portfolio manager assistants are responsible for monitoring the reconciliation of the trades. In this role, they work with the operations staff to assure that the portfolio is properly updated and performance records are accurate. Most firms have separate operations departments that reconcile trades and produce monthly client reports. However, many of the smaller firms require their portfolio assistants to perform the operations function as well. You should be aware of this, and clarify the exact job responsibilities when applying and interviewing for the job.

Portfolio assistants also participate in the process of client service, although the proportion of time spent in this area depends on the type of client being served. For instance, an assistant to a mutual fund portfolio manager would spend very little time on client service. Institutional and high-net-worth portfolio managers have fewer clients and they meet with them once or twice a year. Intermittently, their clients require vast and detailed investment reports and market commentaries. While marketing helps prepare these formal presentations, the portfolio manager assistant plays a crucial role in collecting economic and market data for the investment commentary and portfolio analysis sections of the report.

The position requires a person who understands capital markets, is capable of meeting deadlines and enjoys working on multiple projects simultaneously. The downside is that the reporting and operational components of the job have a quick learning curve and then become repetitive. Furthermore, it is not the best place to learn how to really value companies. Rather, you are being exposed to the years of experience that the portfolio manager possesses. Most important, portfolio manager assistants receive the benefit of seeing a broad picture of investing money across several industries, whereas research assistants typically get exposure to one component or sector. All in all, in the right setting, the position is a great introduction to the industry and a worthwhile apprenticeship to pursue.

Portfolio Manager Assistant

Uppers	Downers
• Broad exposure to the industry	• Less formal training process
• Reasonable working hours	• Some operations work
• Direct exposure to portfolio managers	• Repetitive assignments

Find investment management firm profiles, the Vault Investment Management Careers Message board, and open positions in investment management at the Vault Finance Career Channel:

http://finance.vault.com

We also recommend these Vault guides:

• Vault Career Guide to Investment Banking
• Vault Career Guide to Venture Capital
• Vault Career Guide to Accounting
• Vault Guide to Finance Interviews
• Vault Guide to Advanced and Quantitative Finance Interviews

Investment Research

CHAPTER 6

The investment research segment is responsible for generating recommendations to portfolio managers on companies and industries that they follow. Similar to the portfolio management segment, there are three potential positions: senior research analyst, investment research associate and investment research assistant. Senior research analysts typically have 2 to 4 years of post-MBA research experience. Research associates are usually recent MBA graduates, while assistants are recent college graduates.

Senior Research Analyst

Senior research analysts are investment experts in their given industry focus. An equity analyst covers stocks; a fixed income analyst covers bonds.

Their role is to predict the investment potential of the companies in their sector. For instance, take an equity analyst covering computer hardware companies, including Apple Computer. The analyst would be responsible for predicting Apple's future earnings and cash flow, and comparing the fair value of Apple to the expectations of the stock market. To do this, the analyst would build a financial model that included all of the potential variables to derive Apple's earnings and appropriate value (e.g., sales growth and business costs, as well as research and development).

A fixed income analyst focusing on telecom, for example, might be looking at a new high-yield corporate bond issued by Qwest. The main thing the analyst will be looking for is Qwest's ability to pay off that loan – the amount of the bond. The analyst will look at historical cash flows, project future cash flows and look at other debt obligations that might be more senior to the new bond. This will tell the analyst the likelihood that Qwest will be able to pay off the bond.

Analysts spend a considerable amount of time attending industry conferences, meeting with company management and analyzing industry supply and demand trends to derive business forecasts. Many analysts follow 20 to 30 companies and must be an expert on each.

An important part of a senior research analyst's job is to convey their recommendations to the portfolio management teams. Therefore, senior analysts spend considerable time presenting to portfolio managers and issuing investment reports. Because of this, senior research analysts must be articulate and persuasive in their convictions in order to earn respect within the firm.

Senior research analysts typically have served as investment research associates for 2 to 4 years, post MBA or CFA, before assuming their position. If successful in their role, many senior analysts move into portfolio management roles later in their careers.

Investment Research Associate

This is the role for most MBAs or those with equivalent experience. Essentially, investment research associates have the same responsibilities as senior research analysts with one exception: associates are given smaller industries to follow. Typically, the industry assigned to an associate is a component of a broader sector that is already being analyzed by a senior analyst. For instance, a research associate might be assigned HMOs and work closely with the senior analyst in charge of insurance companies.

The associate analyst creates investment recommendations in the same manner as a senior analyst. In general, new associates spend several weeks familiarizing themselves with their industry by reading industry papers, journals and textbooks, and attending industry conferences. A large percentage of a research analyst's time is spent monitoring industry and company trends to predict financial results for the company. Therefore, research associates are constantly speaking with management, customers and suppliers to gauge the current status of the company they are analyzing. Armed with financial models and fundamental company analysis, they develop investment recommendations that they distribute to the firm's portfolio managers.

One of the greatest challenges for a new associate is the steepness of the learning curve. Portfolio managers don't have the patience or the luxury to allow an analyst to be uninformed or consistently incorrect. New associates work extremely hard building trust with portfolio managers.

Obviously, financial acumen and quantitative skills are a must for a research associate, but communication skills are also critical. Research associates need to be able to clearly and persuasively communicate their investment recommendations. These associates must also be able to respond to detailed inquiries from portfolio managers that challenge their ideas – which requires a strong tact and a great deal of patience. Furthermore, associates need to be energetic, diligent and intellectually curious.

Research associates are usually promoted to larger industries within 2 to 4 years of joining the firm.

Investment Research Associate

Uppers	Downers
• Autonomy and creative independence	• Long hours (60+ hours/week)
• High level of responsibility	• Steep learning curve
• Fewer hours than the sell-side (55-75 hours/week)	• Always being graded on your recommendations
• Pays well	• Must earn the respect of portfolio managers
• Typically a collegial environment	

Investment Research Assistant

Investment research assistants work with senior research analysts to help in developing investment recommendations to portfolio managers. Recent college graduates will spend, on average, 2 to 4 years in this role before returning to business school. However, some of the most successful assistants are often promoted directly to research associate (most of these fast-trackers will have completed their CFA while working as an assistant).

The investment research assistant is responsible for helping to monitor the industry and changes within companies covered in the industry, and for updating financial models accordingly. Assistants collect data for industry data services, company conference calls and surveys. For instance, in the previous Apple Computer example, the assistant would be collecting data about consumer demand and input prices for semiconductors. Additionally, the assistant provides support to the senior analyst in the construction of recommendation reports sent out to the portfolio managers. Specifically, the assistant updates charts and modifies numerical sections of the report.

While some of the work is routine and the hours are long, assistants are sitting next to, and learning from, the intellectual capital of the firm. A good analyst will teach you the ropes, including the intangibles behind analyzing companies, financial valuation and industry knowledge.

The role of investment research assistant requires a high level of quantitative knowledge. Primarily, a basic working knowledge of accounting, financial markets, financial analysis and statistics is needed for this position. Aside from a strong quantitative background, research assistants need to be detail oriented, analytical problem solvers, diligent, and superior communicators. Generally, firms are looking for finance or accounting majors for these jobs, but engineers and science majors are also coveted for technology and health care related industries.

Investment Research Assistant

Uppers	Downers
• Great quantitative experience	• Long hours (60+ hours/week)
• Most portfolio managers were once in research	• Lots of independent time in front of the computer
• Gain industry expertise	• Repetitive assignments
• Pays well	
• Typically a collegial environment	

Marketing and Sales

CHAPTER 7

Increasingly, as the industry grows and matures, investment management companies are focusing on professional marketing and sales as a point of differentiation – especially on the institutional side of the business.

Traditionally, marketing and sales have been more or less an afterthought: much of the marketing and sales work was performed by investment professionals. This is no longer the case, however, and firms are increasingly building teams of dedicated marketing and sales professionals.

Because sales and marketing professionals are typically required to be fluent in all of the investment products, these positions create a great opportunity to learn about the various investment styles that clients demand. This area is a great career opportunity for those who are interested in asset management but don't want to be the investment decision maker.

If your goal is to use sales and marketing as a stepping stone to the investment side, make it a point to network early on with investment professionals and prove yourself at your current job before making it known that you want to make the switch, and work toward developing the quantitative skills needed for the investment positions.

Below is a broad description of the positions that exist in the institutional marketing and sales segment.

Marketing and Sales Manager

Marketing and sales managers are responsible for identifying new clients, presenting the firm's investment capabilities to new and existing clients, solidifying new relationships and servicing existing clients. As was previously discussed, institutional clients are demanding. The search process for being selected to manage an institution's assets is rigorous and lengthy – it could take up to several years. Asset managers make several presentations, and institutions conduct extensive due diligence.

Once an investment management firm is hired, the marketing and sales managers serve in a client relationship capacity. In this role, they arrange semi-annual portfolio reviews, prepare presentations and assure that the proper reporting procedures are followed. Furthermore, managers work to broaden client relationships by introducing institutions to additional investment products offered by the firm. To do this, sales managers must be constantly aware of their clients' needs. They do this by reading current news about their clients and meeting with them on a regular basis. Additionally, sales managers educate themselves on the various products that clients might be interested in. This is where the marketing managers come in: after sales managers identify a client's product need, marketing managers determine how best to present the product to the client.

Marketing and sales managers are MBA graduates or those with equivalent experience. Increasingly, many of these managers are acquiring CFA degrees as client sophistication has increased.

Marketing or Sales Associate

Marketing and sales associates are typically recent college graduates. The positions are quite similar, although they are traditionally segmented by different types of organization.

Marketing associates assist in creating portfolio review presentations and in developing promotional presentations for potential new clients. They are traditionally segmented by investment product type such as equity or fixed income.

Sales associates assist in answering RFPs (request for proposals) issued by institutions seeking to hire new investment managers. Additionally, associates assist senior client servicing officials in maintaining and expanding client relationships. Sales associates are traditionally segmented by client type – public pension funds, corporate pension funds, endowments and foundations.

Marketing or Sales Associate

Uppers	Downers
• Broad knowledge of all of the investment products in the marketplace	• Difficult to jump to the investment side
• Great professional atmosphere for people that like the industry, but don't want to be the investment decision maker	• Limited focus on building quantitative skills
• Less hierarchical career path than the investment side	• Repetitive assignments
• More entry level jobs than the investment side	
• Lots of client interaction	

Alternative Entry Points

Don't give up if one of the typical positions isn't available for you – these are difficult jobs to get. If you are having no luck getting positions with portfolio management or investment research teams, there are many other alternatives to pursue that will better position you to reapply with only a year or two of additional experience. Below are descriptions of some of the best options to consider.

1. Buy-side trading and operations: As we suggested in the previous section, many smaller firms integrate trade reconciliation and reporting with the portfolio manager assistant position. However, the larger firms typically have extensive back-office operation teams. These trading and operations personnel process the investment trades done by portfolio managers.

In general, the positions include mutual fund accounting, trade confirmation, trade reconciliation and report processing. The job really doesn't prepare you directly for the investment side of the business, but it does afford you the opportunity to get to know people in the business and build goodwill with the asset management firm. Moving from the operations side to the investment side of the firm is challenging (therefore, this is only a suggested option for recent college graduates with limited experience). To improve your chances, we would suggest considering firms that encourage this type of maturation process and integrate operations into the investment business – many firms create a clear separation.

2. Sell-side investment research: Many buy-side investment professionals come form the sell-side. It is a great place to learn to do analysis, generate financial models and construct investment reports. The quantitative skills and knowledge of the overall investment business makes former sell-side people desirable to asset management firms.

3. Investment consulting: These are the firms that advise institutions, high-net-worth investors and 401(k) plans on appropriate diversification strategies and which asset managers to hire. At the entry level, you will assist on manager searches and data collection for multiple investment styles. It is a good introduction to the different firms and the dynamics of the industry as a whole.

4. Take the CFA Exam (Chartered Financial Analyst): This is a three-part exam that tests your knowledge in financial accounting, statistics, investment analysis, economics and ethics, among other subjects. The exam is offered in the late spring and is taken over the course of three years. The CFA is becoming a standard for the industry and many people begin the process prior to even entering the industry. It is not a prerequisite to getting an investment job, but working toward achieving it can certainly give you a leg up on your peers, especially pre-MBA candidates.

Days in the Life

It's tough to visualize what a working day as an investment management professional is like if you haven't already worked in the field. To give you a better idea of what it's actually like, here's a look at some "typical" days in the life of investment management professionals we spoke with.

Investment Research Associate, Major Mutual Fund Firm

7:00 a.m.: Arrive at the office.

7:01: Read *The Wall Street Journal* and *Financial Times,* paying particular attention to articles about the industry you follow.

7:30: Listen to morning call voice mails from sell-side analysts. ("Each sell-side firm has a morning meeting, and the highlights are sent via the institutional salesperson to their asset management clients.")

8:00: Attend the morning investment meeting. ("Most firms have a daily meeting where all analyst and portfolio managers gather to relay new information, initiate stock recommendations and discuss current market changes.")

9:00: Listen to a company's investment conference call ("particularly during earnings reposting season. These calls usually include updates from the CEO and CFO on operating performance, strategic initiatives and future company expectations.")

9:45: Open the stack of reports in your inbox. Study the latest industry press and investment literature to identify new trends that may impact the companies you follow.

10:30: Phone industry analysts and company management with follow-up questions.

11:00: Meet with your research associate to discuss potential changes that need to be made to financial models and investment recommendations based on new information gathered during the morning's activities

12:00 p.m.: Eat lunch while attending an industry conference or a meeting with sell-side analysts. ("These are great ways to gather new insights and meet with industry players in a less formal setting.")

1:30: Continue working on the written investment analysis of the company you are going to initiate coverage on the next day. ("This is the culmination of a two-week process in which you met with management of the company, visited the two largest manufacturing facilities, spoke with large customers of the company and conducted surveys on the demand expectations of their new product line.")

2:45: Take a phone call from a senior portfolio manager who wants to discuss in more detail the investment report you issued last week on XYZ Company. ("Specifically, he wants additional support for why you believe earnings will fall 12 percent when the company has stated they expect only a 6-8 percent decline.")

3:15: Sit down to write the final recommendation summary for the company you will initiate coverage on the next morning.

4:00: Review the day's trading activity to see how your industry performed, again paying particular attention to the company you are initiating coverage on. ("If the investment team likes the idea, they will be paying close attention to the recent trading performance of the stock.")

4:30: Meet with your research associate to put the finishing touches on the PowerPoint presentation that you will use to pitch the new stock the following morning. ("You identify a few changes to the slides and decide to cut out a few pages, remember that portfolio managers do not want to be inundated with information; they only want the necessary facts and the pertinent details that support your recommendation.")

5:30: Check the newswires and first-call notes for any after-hours company news.

6:00: Head to the gym ("for a quick workout to clear your head. Hopefully there is a workout facility in the building.")

7:00: Return to the office to run through the final PowerPoint slides and to make sure the initiation report is on the top of each portfolio manager's inbox.

7:45: Leave for home.

Investment Management Associate, J.P. Morgan Fleming (J.P. Morgan Chase Asset Management)

8:00 a.m. Arrive at work.

8:01: Morning meeting.

8:30: Check voice mail; return phone calls.

9:00: Call research analysts and discuss earnings projections.

9:30: Stock market opens.

10:00: Meetings with analysts begin. ("It may be the beginning of up to eight straight hours of meetings.")

1:00 p.m.: Eat lunch at your desk.

1:30: Review new issues coming to market this week. ("Looking at new issues takes up the bulk of your time.")

2:30: Keep track of existing portfolio holdings.

3:30: Drop in on investment conference; listen to two 45-minute presentations including a 30-minute presentation by company management with 15 minutes of Q&A. ("Industry conferences are the most efficient way to quickly learn about several different companies and decide whether they're worth your attention.")

5:30: Return to office; prepare for industry conference tomorrow by reading several research reports and some trade publications.

6:45: Take train home.

Investment Banking Research Associate, Deutsche Bank Equity Research

6:30 a.m.: Wake up. ("Unfortunately, working in research, you have to get up pretty early.")

7:30: Arrive at work. ("First thing I do is check NewsEdge, CNN and CNBC, see what's going on, what's happening politically to affect my coverage. You can listen to the morning call, which starts everyday at 7:15 and lasts until 8, but I only listen if my boss will be on it, or if there's breaking news in our sector.")

8:00: Coffee with boss and group. ("We'll sit down and talk about the news, discuss the market and plan our day.")

9:00: Listen to earnings call (company you cover releases earnings, quarterly or annual), followed by Q&A with the firm that released the call. ("If you have crucial questions to ask a company, now you have to pose them in a public forum because of the regulatory concerns.")

11:00: Begin to write first call note (your firm's investment thesis on the company that released the call). Open up Excel and update financial model for note.

U.S. sales force starts to call. ("Clients will call asking you what you think of the results of the call – Do you think estimates will rise? What's the stock going to do? Basically, we tell them what we think thus far – where the company's weaknesses and strengths are.")

("Quarterly earnings releases take 2-3 pages. If the investment thesis is new, we create new text. I f we stay with the same viewpoint, we still have to add new content to support that viewpoint. We aim to get the note out before the end of the trading day. If the call takes place during the day, and you're a good analyst, your note should be out at least by first thing in the morning.")

12:00 p.m.: Lunch. ("Almost everyday, we go out as a team: We usually grab a salad, bring it back and sit at my boss' desk to get caught up. And we don't just talk about business.")

1:00: Finalize marketing presentation for an investor meeting with a potential client (company you might cover). ("Put in detail behind the company's industry, our viewpoints, public trading performance, historical valuations, how they compare, snapshots. Put in a lot of elaborate charts and graphs. The thing is more a take home pack, rather than an outline for the meeting.")

2:00: Meeting out of office. ("At the meetings, associates are almost spectators. They only talk if somebody asks something like, 'Can I clarify what the percent of geographic sales is?' Meetings usually include a salesperson, an analyst and an associate on our side.")

4:00: Back in office. Continue on first call. ("After you update it, you show it to your analyst [your boss], who will ask you to add some things. This then gets sent out in hard copy format. It may take a while to move it through the necessary compliance channels and get it out the door.")

5:00: Boss leaves.

7:30: Leave for the day. ("The earliest I usually leave is 7:30 or 8. In the summer, though, I can leave earlier. And during earnings season, I usually leave later, because there's can be two or three earnings releases in one day, so you have to get that many first call notes out each day. It can get stressful: three notes, three models – and fielding clients from everywhere.")

Investment Banking Equity Research Associate, Salomon Smith Barney

7:00 a.m.: Get on the subway and read *The Wall Street Journal*. ("I focus on news that's relevant to the companies I cover.")

8:00: Arrive at the office. Look at Reuters to see if there's any breaking news on the companies that you cover. ("Once an hour, all day, I'm checking Reuters for breaking news on my companies. If there's negative news, institutional investor calls start pouring in regarding the effect of the news on the stock.")

8:15: Call the investor relations department at the company for which news came out in order to get their take on it. If there's no breaking news, begin work on ongoing projects such as an industry research report. ("I'll usually have a few piles of projects on my desk.")

8:45: Meet with equity research team, which consists of one senior analyst ("who might be on the road"), one MBA associate, one undergraduate research assistant, and one administrative assistant. ("With respect to effects of negative news, the team must form a unified opinion on a situation. Once we're all on the same page, we start to handle client calls.")

9:15: Write a "global alert" on the news to be sent to sales force worldwide.

9:45: Handle client calls ("their inquiries into the news").

11:30: Meet with team regarding ongoing projects.

12:00 p.m.: Go out to lunch or eat at the firm's cafeteria.

12:30: Return phone calls. Focus on ongoing projects.

1:30: Afternoon team meeting. ("Checking in with the boss. It's important that our team communicates effectively.")

2:00: Downtime. Work on ongoing projects.

4:00: Meet with a company that wants your firm to cover it.

6:00: Order dinner.

6:30: Dinner arrives.

8:00: Head home.

"We don't sit in the corner and just crank out spread sheets. That misperception about research bothers me. Our job is to offer our perspective on stocks to institutional clients. You must have strong verbal and written communication skills. Through morning calls and phone calls we have to communicate our perspective to institutional clients. Sales people and traders understand our business better than investment bankers. Although equity analysts have come under fire recently – with the rise and fall of the legendary analysts – overall, research analysts today are in a much different position than before."

– Salomon Smith Barney investment research associate

GETTING HIRED

Chapter 9: Targeting Your Job Search

Chapter 10: The Interview

Targeting Your
Job Search

Getting the Interview

Once you understand the different types of firms, components of the business and types of positions available, you can begin to target your search. In this chapter, we'll focus on the different types of firms and their hiring processes.

On-campus recruiting

If you're just graduating college or business school, you might have a chance to interview with the larger asset management companies on campus, but don't expect your search to end there. The number of jobs that these firms offer is very limited, so competition for these spots is high. Additionally, very few of the mid- and small-size firms recruit actively on campus. In a good year, a top MBA school might have 20 investment management firms – most likely only the largest in the industry – recruiting on campus. In other years, though, the same school might have just a handful recruiting; it's not uncommon that a firm will recruit one year, and not the next. Beyond the top 10 or so asset managers, most firms are relatively unknown to those outside the industry, and there are quite a few of these lesser-known firms. As a result, many job opportunities exist. However, these positions aren't always that easy to locate.

Off-campus searching

Ultimately, the investment management job search requires diligence and perseverance. Like any independent job search, your best bet is to schmooze and network. We have found that the best resources include school alumni databases, previous work contacts, family friends and personal associations. However, do not hesitate to use cold calls to solicit contact with the firms that interest you. A strong cover letter, exceptional professional and educational background and persistence are often rewarded with an opportunity to interview with the company.

Another resource is the AIMR (Association for Investment Management and Research), headquartered in Charlottesville, Va. The AIMR is an association of 50,000 investment professionals and educators in over 100 countries. The organization holds seminars on investment management topics, oversees the

CFA exam, offers continuing education courses and hosts social events. AIMR chapters in larger cities, such as New York and Boston, meet frequently, often once a week. Chapters in smaller cities meet less often. Students can attend AIMR meetings, which require a $30 entrance fee, to network and learn more about the industry. For more information on AIMR, including its newsletters and various publications such as *Financial Analyst Journal*, check out the association's website, www.aimr.com.

What they want

Because it's difficult for MBAs, and even more difficult for undergrads, to enter asset management through the front door, several slide into the industry through the side. Although there's no common professional background that defines asset management success (and, in fact, diverse backgrounds are great benefits to investment management companies), lateral hires typically come from jobs in I-banking or management consulting, or from respected *Fortune* 500 corporations such as GE or Johnson & Johnson.

In investment banking and accounting, you'll gain quantitative abilities (such as company valuation and financial statement analysis) similar to those used in asset management. Investment managers also like candidates with management consulting – especially strategic consulting – backgrounds, because consultants usually have obtained the skill to quickly immerse themselves in and learn about an industry. Marketing research professionals from large corporations are also highly regarded in asset management, because they have expertise in learning about different companies and how they compete in the marketplace.

Where do you fit?

Before embarking on your job search, you must ask yourself the following questions: Do I want to go into equity or fixed income? Am I interested in growth investing or value investing? What investment style suits me? What kind of research do I want to do? What size firm do I want? Where do I want to live? Answering all these questions will not only allow you to narrow down what could be an extremely exhaustive search, but will also help you at interview time – because firms will definitely ask you, "Why us?"

Who are the Asset Management Employers? A Basic Breakdown

Large generalist firms

As we discussed earlier, the industry has gone through dramatic changes over the last 20 years. Consolidation and the focus on globalization have transformed the industry from its fragmented "specialist" structure. Today, asset management is part of nearly every financial services firm, both in the U.S. and abroad. For the sake of simplicity, we have assigned asset managers to five general categories, and listed a few examples of each.

Category	Examples
Pure Investment Management Companies	Fidelity, Vanguard, AMVSECAP
Divisions of Investment Banks	JP Morgan, Merrill Lynch
Divisions of Global Commercial Banks	Citigroup, Barclays
Divisions of Domestic Commercial Banks	Mellon, Northern Trust
Divisions of Insurance Companies	Prudential, Putnam

As you can see, most of the large investment management firms are actually divisions of broader financial services companies. However, in many cases, the asset management divisions are run as entirely separate autonomous entities. In other cases, the parent predicates the culture and focus of the business. As you explore career options in the industry, do your homework about the firm's structure and understand how the division operates.

Specialist firms

While the industry has shifted somewhat away from specialist firms, their role continues to be in demand because of the specific expertise they can provide. Today, there are nearly 500 firms that manage between $1 billion and $30 billion. These firms are located throughout the country and usually have relatively smaller staffs and vastly different cultures. Below, we have included a small sampling of "specialists" with a variety of investment focuses.

Specialist Firms	Headquarters	AUM's as of 12/31/00 ($ billions)	Investment Focus
Payden & Rygel	Los Angeles, CA	$35.00	Active Fixed Income
Montag & Caldwell	Atlanta, GA	$29.10	U.S. Active Equities
Barrow, Hanley, Mewhinney, & Strauss	Dallas, TX	$27.80	U.S. Active Equities
Bessemer Trust	New York, NY	$27.60	High Net Worth – All Investments
Oechsle International	Boston, MA	$17.70	International Active Equities
Dwight Asset Management	Burlington, VT	$13.60	U.S. Fixed Income
Boston Partners Asset Management	Boston, MA	$10.90	U.S. Active Equities
DSI International	Norwalk, CT	$5.90	U.S. Equity Enhanced Index
Rhumbline Advisors	Boston, MA	$4.70	U.S. Passive Equities
Driehaus Capital Management	Chicago, IL	$4.50	Active Equities

Source: Pension & Investments, May 2001 edition

Generally, the smaller firms do not actively recruit. This means it's up to you to target each firm, research its specialty and contact them directly. A great resource is *Pension & Investments'* annual issue on "The Leading Money Managers." Additionally, *Nelson's Investment Guide* lists investment managers by state and asset classes, and provides telephone numbers and e-mail addresses.

Who are the Asset Management Employers? A Closer Look

The investment industry is a vast one, encompassing thousands of firms and tens of thousands of investment groups within corporations, unions, foundations, schools and government institutions. How can you determine whether a particular firm is the right one for you to join? First, you must understand the kinds of firms within the business and how they tend to hire.

For insider profiles on Fidelity, Putnam Investments, T. Rowe Price and other top investment management firms, go to the Vault Finance Career Channel at http://finance.vault.com.

Vault company information is based on surveys and interviews of actual employees. Also on Vault, find insider profiles on investment banks, commercial banks and other top finance employers.

Tier 1 Complexes

Tier 1 complexes are mutual fund families that offer a complete or nearly complete range of products. They serve significant numbers of retail, institutional and high-net-worth customers, and will have at least $100 billion under management. These firms are well known throughout the industry.

Examples

- Fidelity Investments
- Putnam Investments
- T. Rowe Price
- MFS
- The Capital Group of Companies
- Scudder

Hiring

These firms hire almost exclusively through recruiting at top MBA programs or raiding other Tier 1 or Tier 2 firms. Some will hire BA candidates, but generally only from a top school. Inexperienced hires will be brought on as research assistants/associates (if without a graduate degree) or as junior research analysts (with a graduate degree).

Uppers	Downers
• Exit opportunities, both at graduate schools and within the industry • High pay • Superior access to companies and sell-side analysts • Firm's diverse product lines insulate against downturn in your industry	• Bureaucracy • Internal politics • Extensive travel required

Top-Tier Boutiques

Top-tier boutiques are firms that specialize in a particular type of instrument, industry sector or style. They are nationally or internationally recognized for their expertise in that specialty. A top-tier boutique will have between $500 million to $50 billion under management.

Examples

• Real Estate – Cohen & Steers, Aldrich Eastman Waltch

• Fixed Income – PIMCO, BlackRock

• Technology – Pequot Capital Management, Weiss Peck & Greer, Firsthand

Hiring

Top-tier boutiques hire in a similar fashion to tier 1 complexes. However, if their specialty is currently out of favor, an especially persistent but atypical candidate can sometimes obtain a position at a top-tier boutique.

Uppers	Downers
• Exit opportunities, both at graduate schools and within the industry • Superior access to companies and sell-side analysts • High pay	• Occasional lack of support staff • Extensive travel required

Tier 2 Complexes

Tier 2 complexes are large fund complexes that have a complete or nearly complete product line. However, they are not regarded as highly as Tier 1 complexes or top-tier boutiques. They will often be attached to a bank (whether commercial or investment), insurance company or other financial conglomerate. Tier 2 complexes will serve mainly retail and high-net-worth clients.

Examples

• Franklin Templeton

• AmEx Financial Advisors

• Van Kampen

Hiring

Tier 2 complexes are often scattered in their hiring – hiring internally, recruiting at the undergraduate level at local universities and at the graduate level at both local and Top 20 universities.

Uppers	Downers
• Superior access to companies and sell-side analysts • Firm's diverse product lines insulate against downturn in your industry • Good pay	• Bureaucracy • Internal politics • Extensive travel required

Old-Line Firms

Old-line firms are firms that often were started in the 1930s (or even before). They are generally value/fixed-income shops and focus on capital preservation. They will have a mix of old-money very-high-net-worth clients and local institutions.

Examples

• Dodge & Cox

• Loomis Sayles Stein

• Roe & Farnham

Hiring

OLFs hire at Top 10/15 MBA programs. Occasionally, they may also hire laterals from other (value-oriented) firms that are located in the same city.

Uppers	Downers
• Exit opportunities, both at graduate schools and within the industry • Superior access to companies and sell-side analysts • Good pay • Stable firms, positive (though conservative) cultures	• Bureaucracy • Firm's stodgy philosophy may not appeal to you • Firm expects you to stay with them for many years and structures pay and advancement accordingly

Universities, Foundations, Pension Plans

These are (generally) tax-exempt pools of money. In most cases, the great majority of assets is outsourced to various outside top firms. The investment staff at these institutions selects and monitors these outside managers. Small portions of the assets can be managed internally.

Examples

- Stanford Management Company
- Ford Foundation
- CalPERS

Hiring

The top-tier institutions prefer to hire recent MBA graduates who have spent a number of years (post-MBA) at a premier buy-side or sell-side firm, but who would like to reduce their working hours.

Uppers	Downers
• Exit opportunities, both at graduate schools and within the industry • High job security • Great benefits • Less stressful environment and culture	• Bureaucracy • Focus on asset allocation and monitoring, not in-house management • Relatively low pay • Difficult to get active management jobs due to lack of experience

Venture Capital Funds and Hedge Funds

Venture capital is closer to investment or commercial banking than investment management, in that the main function of a venture capital firm (often called a VC) is to sell its money to high-quality potential entrepreneurs. An investment manager, however, focuses on investing in public equities, not on selling money. (For more information on careers in venture capital, get the *Vault Career Guide to Venture Capital*.)

Hedge funds are very similar to mutual funds and investment advisory firms. The fee structure is different (and extremely rewarding to the partners of a hedge fund) but functionally, below the partner level, employees at hedge funds do similar jobs and will be paid equivalently to employees at other mutual funds or investment advisory firms. Hedge fund jobs are not necessarily more prestigious than other opportunities available. More important, the industry generally does not truly distinguish between a hedge fund specializing in, say, energy and a mutual fund that does so. Each fund will be judged according to performance, size, reputation and quality of personnel, not on its ownership structure. Since hedge funds are relatively small (the largest hedge fund families manage roughly $10 billion), they are simply classified as whatever rank of boutique they are.

Is This Firm Right for Me?

Unlike most other industries, the investment management industry encompasses literally thousands of firms, most of which either do not advertise themselves or are even legally barred from doing so (hedge funds, for example). Much of the time, you are dealing with a job search in which your potential future employers are unknown entities to you. So what sources and criteria should you use when evaluating a potential employer?

1. Firm web site: Staff bios – One of the most helpful portions of an investment management firm's web site is the staff bio section. This is the premier consideration in evaluating a firm. If the staff is good, you will likely have, at minimum, a reasonable experience there. If the staff is weak or poor, you will likely have a sub-par experience there.

How to evaluate staff bios: Two things to look at are the staff's experience and education. At minimum, all principals should have significant experience at top, recognizable buy-side or sell-side operations. Also, most or all of the principals should have degrees (both undergraduate and graduate) from top universities. If some of the principals have non-buy-side experience, it should be at a recognized company or institution. Most of the firm's analysts should have similar backgrounds as well (though, obviously, less experience in terms of years and positions held).

Big warning signs include: 1. None (or few) of the principals has significant experience at a top firm. 2. None (or few) of the principals has a graduate degree from a top university. 3. Analysts have weak academic and/or work backgrounds. No full analyst should have less than three years of experience. 4. Any signs of nepotism. 5. Lists of degrees from unrecognizable universities and/or work experience at unrecognizable firms. 6. Missing periods in bios.

2. Money under management – If the firm's web site does not tell you how much money the firm manages, this information should be obtainable at either the *Nelson's Directory of Investment Managers* or *Pensions & Investments* web sites. If the firm is not in either resource, this is also a warning sign. For a hedge fund, $200 million under management is a good general mark of a fund with a healthy amount of money under management. For regular buy-side firms, firms with significantly less than $500 million should be viewed cautiously.

The investment management business is one where you derive your profits from the amount of money you manage. Hedge funds also gain a portion of the profits they achieve. Any good manager with significant experience at a top firm can walk out the door with commitments of, at minimum, $100 million. Some have walked out with commitments of $500 million to $1 billion. Therefore, a firm that cannot break the $200 million figure just does not have the right staff needed to compete.

3. Whose money do they manage? – You want to join the smartest firm you can. How can you tell whether a firm is smart and will be able to grow? Evaluate the firm's clientele. The smartest clients in the business are the university endowments, large foundations, certain smart corporate pension plans, the sharper state pension plans (especially CalPERS, Ohio State Board of Investments, Wisconsin and Virginia) and some funds of funds (a mutual fund that invests in other mutual funds). Not only do these institutions have fine internal staffs with large budgets to investigate potential managers, but they are advised by numerous consulting firms that also research money managers. Not only will these institutions generally select top-rate managers but, if these managers perform, the institutions have much larger amounts to give them. It is a serious negative if the firm has not been able to attract any of these investors. It means either the staff does not have the level of experience and education to gain these institutions' trust, or their product and/or investment strategies are unappealing, ill-formed or incomprehensible.

The remaining potential client bases are retail and high-net-worth (HNW) investors. Those with retail investment clientele run mutual funds; those that cater to HNW individuals run individual accounts.

How do you find out about the firm's clientele? Ask them, then check their answers against both *Nelson's* and *Pensions & Investments* and search the Internet for manager announcements (when a public pension plan puts money with a new manager, this information is published).

You should target firms that best fit your ideal working environment. The best resources for learning this information are company web sites and through networking with employees of the respective firms. (For more information, check out Vault's insider company profiles and message boards.)

Insurance Companies

Insurance companies often manage extraordinarily large sums of money. This money is derived from policy payments and set aside against potential claims. Insurance companies have historically invested mainly in high-grade fixed-income instruments.

Examples

- State Farm
- Allstate
- Cigna

Hiring

Insurance companies generally hire investment staff from local universities. Historically, insurance companies have been unable to attract many candidates of Top 20 MBA programs. Insurance firms will hire at both the MBA and BA levels.

Uppers	Downers
• High job security	• Bureaucracy
• Great benefits	• Focus on high-grade fixed-income
• Less stressful environment and culture	• Low pay
• Willing to hire non-Ivy candidates	• Low prestige
• Good learning environment	• Extremely conservative investment styles

The Interview

In this chapter, we will explore the most common questions asked of candidates during job interviews. We have segmented the questions into three types: background, analytical/quantitative and personality/fit.

Preparing for the Interview

It is common for candidates to underestimate the importance of preparation for an interview. Interviewers are smart, well prepared and likely to be interviewing many candidates for very few positions. Therefore, the time spent getting ready for the interview may separate the candidates that get the job from those that get the "ding."

The place to start is getting to know the company. Do your research on the firm's history, business strategy, operating structure and financial performance. You do not need to have contacts at the company to gather this information. Some great resources include: company web sites, company annual reports, sell-side analyst reports, business newspapers and magazines, and industry publications such as *Institutional Investor*, *Pensions & Investments*, *Bloomberg* magazine and *The Journal of Portfolio Management*. In addition, check out *Nelson's Directory of Investment Managers* or *Nelson's Directory of Investment Research*, both of which are thick reference books to firms in the industry found in most school libraries. Articulating to the interviewer that you know about the company helps to exhibit your passion about the position and diligence in your preparation.

Next, you need to plan how to position yourself during the interview. Think of an interview as a sales presentation and the product you are marketing is yourself. You need to establish the critical points of your background and character that will make you the ideal candidate for the job. In doing this we suggest the following:

• Know every detail on your resume

• Prepare answers to the common questions detailed below

• Expect the unexpected

• Practice repeatedly

Background Questions

1) What was your most significant accomplishment to date?

It is important when answering this question to focus on an accomplishment that highlights the skills needed to be successful in the specific position you are applying for. For instance, when interviewing for an investment research associate or assistant position it is important to mention an accomplishment that required keen quantitative skills, problem solving ability and success as a team member. Be sure when answering this question that you provide tangible and measurable results to your accomplishment. For example, "…as a result, the company increased revenue by 10 percent," or "…as a result, the portfolio's performance exceeded its benchmark."

2) Tell me about a recent professional experience when you had to convince someone to accept your idea.

The interviewer wants to know how effective you are at articulating your recommendations and defending your opinions. This is an important part of being an investment professional. A great way to answer this question is to state whom you were trying to convince and why they opposed your point of view. Then highlight how you overcame this. For example, "…I supported my analysis by outlining and measuring the potential risks associated with the project. By clearly comparing the strengths and the weaknesses of the project, my boss saw the merit of investing in the business." Finish the example with the measurable and tangible results of your actions.

3) What was the most important thing you learned in your last job and why did you leave?

For those just graduating school this question is less likely, but for others it is a common question. When answering this question be positive, even if the story did not end happily. Think about how you can link the skills learned in your last job, to the talents needed in the new desired position.

4) Why are you interested in the "buy-side" instead of the "sell-side?"

This question is often asked to gauge your knowledge of the differences between the two sides of the business. Most interviewers are not looking for a specific answer, but rather a reasonable rationale. Acceptable answers might include references to closer interaction with portfolio managers, more input into the investment decisions, and dedicated focus on performing investment analysis (instead of marketing and writing investment reports).

Analytical and Quantitative Questions

The level of difficulty of the analytical interview questions depends on the level of position you are interviewing for. Analytical questions will generally be about stock recommendations and valuation, the economy or financial accounting. Anyone above the assistant level should be prepared to defend his or her knowledge of these aspects of financial analysis.

Stock and bond recommendations and valuation questions

1) How do you go about valuing a company?

There are two generally acceptable answers to this question. One is using a discounted cash flow (DCF) approach and the other is to use a comparable financial multiple analysis. Be sure you know the differences between each and why most analysts don't use a DCF approach in valuing companies. Mainly, they argue that it is very difficult to predict accurate discount rates and terminal values for the company. (In the next section we will outline these two ways of valuing companies.)

Analysts compare their own valuation of a company to the current stock market valuation. If analysts' valuation of the company is greater than the stock market value, then they would typically recommend its purchase.

2) Tell me about a stock that you think would be a good investment today.

You should be prepared to discuss at least one stock during the interview. The interviewer is not interested in your investment opinion, but rather your ability to present a well organized approach. The interviewer, most likely, will want you to keep your stock pitch brief (10 minutes). Therefore, hit the highlights quickly and focus on being persuasive. The steps listed below will assist in preparing a well-articulated thesis for any company.

1) Overview of the company and its competitive position:

- Identify major products and highlight their current market share and growth rates.

- Competitive advantages (i.e., brand equity, first to market, strong management team, substantial free cash flow, innovative product development, strong customer service).

2) Industry analysis:

- Number of competitors.

- Growth of the market – impact of external factors such as the economy and customer demand.

3) Analysis of the company's future prospects (new products, etc.):

- Analyze management's growth strategy.

- Identify business drivers.

- Does the company have the correct product mix to match future customer demand?

- Will earnings grow through cost controls, price increases, or unit sales increase?

4) Investment risks – it is important to quantify the things that can go wrong when determining a proper value for the company:

- Sensitivity to macroeconomic conditions.

- Management secession.

- Regulatory changes.

- Changing operating input prices.

5) Recent financial performance – stocks go up and down based on their performance versus expectations. For instance, if investors expect 25% earnings growth and the company only produces 23%, the stock price will most likely fall:

- Highlight company earnings and sales growth versus the industry and expectations.

- Measure the progress of operating margins.

- Indicate market share gains.

6) Financial valuation of the company (relative to industry comparables):

• Please see the "valuing a company" section of this book.

• Steps 1-5 are incorporated into the financial predictions used for valuing the company.

7) Summarize your investment recommendation:

• Some companies may ask for a full written investment report, so preparing this type of analysis in a written version may be a good idea.

3) A client in the 28% tax bracket has a choice between a tax-free municipal bond yielding 7% and a corporate bond yielding 8.5%. Which should he choose? What would the yield on the corporate bond have to be in order to be equivalent to the tax-free bond?

You have to compare the instruments on the same basis in order to decide. Since the muni bond is tax-free, you have to find the after-tax yield of the corporate bond and compare that with the muni.

Take the corporate bond first and consider a one-year period for simplicity. Suppose the client invested $1,000 and earned 8.5%. Of this 8.5%, 28% will be taxed, so the client's gain is $(1-t)y\$1000 = (1-0.28)0.085*\$1,000 = 61.2$. This is equivalent to a tax-free yield of 6.12%. So, since the yield of the tax-free bond is greater than the after-tax yield of the corporate bond, the client should choose the muni.

To determine the yield that will give parity between the corporate bond and the muni bond, use the formula "after tax yield on corporate = tax free rate" or, $(1-t)y_{corp} = y_{tax-free}$, then $y_{corp} = y_{tax-free}/(1-t)$. For this example, the yield on the corporate bond would have to be $0.07/(1-0.28) = 9.722\%$ in order to be equivalent to the tax-free bond. If corporate bond yields are lower than 9.722%, choose the muni; otherwise, choose the corporate bond since the higher yield will offset the cost of the tax.

4) What would be a good instrument to use to hedge a portfolio of preferred stock?

Since preferred stock is similar to bonds that never mature (perpetual bonds), the best hedging instrument would be a long-maturity, risk-free instrument such as a T-bond option based on long-term treasuries.

5) If you are buying corporate bonds, which is more speculative: A, Aa, Baa or B?

B is the most speculative of these ratings.

6) If a client purchases a 6%, $1,000 bond selling at a yield to maturity of 7%, what is the amount of the semi-annual interest payment?

Yield is unimportant here. It is the coupon payment, 6% of $1,000 each year is $60 or $30 every six months. Don't get confused if the interviewer adds extra information to the question.

7) How can you reduce the risk of a portfolio?

You add instruments for diversification. Hopefully these instruments are not well correlated with each other, so overall they reduce risk. For equities, theoretically, you need about 30 different stocks for efficient diversification. There are many forms of risk: credit risk, liquidity risk, country risk, market risk, firm-specific risk and so on. You can also include hedging instruments: for example, if you own a particular equity, you could buy put options on it.

8) What is a warrant? Do warrants affect a firm's financial ratios such as ROE?

A warrant is a security similar to a call option on a stock, except a warrant usually has a longer life (time until it expires) than a call. Warrants may often be attached to issues of preferred stock or bonds in order to make the issue more attractive to investors, because warrants offer the opportunity for some participation in stock appreciation. When the warrant is exercised, the owner pays the stated strike price in exchange for new shares of common stock. All other things equal, whenever a company's number of common shares outstanding increases, measures such as ROE and EPS should decrease, because shareholders' ownership is diluted.

Economic questions

1) What economic indicators do you think have the greatest impact on the stock/bond markets?

There are many good answers to this question, but the best approach is to discuss economic factors that are currently impacting the market. The interviewer wants to know that you are well informed to current market dynamics.

You should read several leading financial periodicals prior to any interview, such as *The Wall Street Journal*, the *Financial Times*, *The Economist*, and *BusinessWeek*. Articles in these magazines will provide you with the current economic influences on the market.

In general, you should know that investment analysts pay close attention to weekly, monthly, and quarterly economic reports. Announcements of these economic indicators have major impact on equity and bond market performance. The most heavily watched economic reports include:

- **Consumer price index** – measures inflation.

- **Unemployment** – company labor costs and profitability are driven by the level of employment in the market.

- **Gross Domestic Product (GDP)** – measures the growth of the entire domestic economy. Analysts use GDP to forecast the sales levels and profitability growth rates of companies.

- **Unit labor costs** – measures the productivity level of workers.

- **Fed funds rate** – the rate set by the Fed for banks to borrow and lend money to the government. When the Fed cuts rates they are signaling a weak economy and are trying to stimulate borrowing and spending. When the Fed raises rates they are trying to slow the economy by inducing people to save. The Fed is constantly trying to keep the economy from being too hot or too cold.

Well-prepared interviewees will know the current level, past trends and future expectations of each of these indicators.

2) Discuss the trends in the industry that you previously worked in.

This question is designed to gauge your ability to think strategically. In essence, the interviewer is asking if you can identify the:

- Strengths and weaknesses of the industry
- Level of competition
- Regulatory changes
- Impact of economic changes
- New innovations
- Industry threats

Financial accounting questions

1) What is free cash flow?

It measures the cash available after adjusting for capital expenditures. Popular uses of free cash flow are dividends, stock buybacks, acquisitions and investing in new business developments.

Free cash flow is computed from the following financial statement line items:

Net Income
+ Depreciation expenses
+ Amortization of goodwill
+ Year-over-year changes in deferred taxes
− Year-over-year change in net working capital (current assets – current liabilities)
= Cash Flow from Operations

− Net Capital Expenditures
= Free Cash Flow

2) How do you calculate WACC (Weighted average cost of capital)?

Essentially, it is the average cost of obtaining capital from all sources of financing (debt and equity stakeholders). Before determining the weighted average, you must first determine the borrowing rate of each form of financing. Equity cost of capital is found by using CAPM, which is computed as follows:

Cost of Equity = Rf + [B*(Rm − Rf)]

Where:

Rf = Risk Free Rate of the market (t-bills)
B = Beta of the stock
Rm = Historical stock market return

Debt cost of capital (current yield) is often estimated as the company's interest expense divided by its book value of long-term debt.

Once the cost of equity and debt are computed, a weighted average is used to determine the company's WACC. The company's market capitalization is used for the equity portion, while the market value of the company's bonds is used for the debt allocation.

For example, assume that the company's cost of equity was computed as 14% (using CAPM) and the cost of debt was computed as 9%. And assume that the stock market valuation of the company was $10 billion and the market value of the debt was $5 billion. Therefore, the percentage of equity financing would be equal to [$10 billion / ($10 billion + $5 billion)], or 66.7%. Debt financing would account for 33.3% of the overall financing, [$5 billion / ($10 billion + $5 billion)]. Therefore the WACC is:

WACC = [Weight of Equity * Cost of Equity]
+ [Weight of Debt * Cost of Debt]

or

WACC = [66.7% * 14%] + (33.3% * 9%) = **12.34%**

Personality/Fit Questions

---

1) Where do you see yourself in five years?

This question is designed to test the career focus of candidates. When answering this question be certain to have reasonable goals that are well aligned with the firm you are interviewing with. For example, if you were interviewing with a firm that emphasizes a team portfolio management process, you would not want to describe your aspirations for being a star at the firm.

2) What is your greatest reservation about working in asset management?

This is one of those negative questions that you have to be very careful in answering. In essence, the interviewer is asking for your weaknesses. Be certain that your answer does not highlight a fundamental flaw that would be detrimental to your success in the position you are interviewing for. For example, "I am not really good with numbers" or "I don't ever want to work on the weekends."

3) What are you most proud of?

This is a great place to talk about extracurricular activities or personal interests. This helps the interviewer get to know you better. Be prepared to share interesting anecdotes that show a passion for the activities you have pursued. This is also a great place to highlight your abilities as a leader.

Be very prepared. Be very, very prepared.

- Insider guides, including the best-selling Vault Guide to Finance Interviews, the Vault Finance Interviews Practice Guide, the Vault Guide to Advanced and Quantitative Finance Interviews

- Vault's one-on-one Finance Interview Prep, a 1-hour live phone interview coaching session with a Vault expert

Go to the Vault Finance Career Channel at http://finance.vault.com

APPENDIX

Glossary

Valuing a Company

About the Authors

Increase your T/NJ Ratio
(Time to New Job)

Use the Internet's most targeted job search tools for finance professionals.

Vault Finance Job Board

The most comprehensive and convenient job board for finance professionals. Target your search by area of finance, function, and experience level, and find the job openings that you want. No surfing required.

VaultMatch Resume Database

Vault takes match-making to the next level: post your resume and customize your search by area of finance, experience and more. We'll match job listings with your interests and criteria and e-mail them directly to your inbox.

Glossary

Accretive merger: A merger in which the acquiring company's earnings per share increase.

Balance Sheet: One of the four basic financial statements, the Balance Sheet presents the financial position of a company at a given point in time, including Assets, Liabilities, and Equity.

Beta: A value that represents the relative volatility of a given investment with respect to the market.

Bond price: The price the bondholder (the lender) pays the bond issuer (the borrower) to hold the bond (i.e., to have a claim on the cash flows documented on the bond).

Bond spreads: The difference between the yield of a corporate bond and a U.S. Treasury security of similar time to maturity.

Buy-side: The clients of investment banks (mutual funds, pension funds) that buy the stocks, bonds and securities sold by the investment banks. (The investment banks that sell these products to investors are known as the "sell-side.")

Callable bond: A bond that can be bought back by the issuer so that it is not committed to paying large coupon payments in the future.

Call option: An option that gives the holder the right to purchase an asset for a specified price on or before a specified expiration date.

Capital Asset Pricing Model (CAPM): A model used to calculate the discount rate of a company's cash flows.

Commercial bank: A bank that lends (rather than raises) money. For example, if a company wants $30 million to open a new production plant, it can approach a commercial bank like Bank of America or Citibank for a loan. (Increasingly, commercial banks are also providing investment banking services to clients.)

Commercial paper: Short-term corporate debt, typically maturing in nine months or less.

Commodities: Assets (usually agricultural products or metals) that are generally interchangeable with one another and therefore share a common price. For example, corn, wheat and rubber generally trade at one price on commodity markets worldwide.

Common stock: Also called common equity, common stock represents an ownership interest in a company (as opposed to preferred stock, see below). The vast majority of stock traded in the markets today is common, as common stock enables investors to vote on company matters. An individual with 51 percent or more of common shares owned controls a company's decisions and can appoint anyone he/she wishes to the board of directors or to the management team.

Comparable transactions (comps): A method of valuing a company for a merger or acquisition that involves studying similar transactions.

Convertible preferred stock: A relatively uncommon type of equity issued by a company, convertible preferred stock is often issued when it cannot successfully sell either straight common stock or straight debt. Preferred stock pays a dividend, similar to how a bond pays coupon payments, but ultimately converts to common stock after a period of time. It is essentially a mix of debt and equity, and is most often used as a means for a risky company to obtain capital when neither debt nor equity works.

Capital market equilibrium: The principle that there should be equilibrium in the global interest rate markets.

Convertible bonds: Bonds that can be converted into a specified number of shares of stock.

Cost of Goods Sold: The direct costs of producing merchandise. Includes costs of labor, equipment and materials to create the finished product, for example.

Coupon payments: The payments of interest that the bond issuer makes to the bondholder.

Credit ratings: The ratings given to bonds by credit agencies. These ratings indicate the risk of default.

Currency appreciation: When a currency's value is rising relative to other currencies.

Currency depreciation: When a currency's value is falling relative to other currencies.

Currency devaluation: When a currency weakens under fixed exchange rates.

Currency revaluation: When a currency strengthens under fixed exchange rates.

Default premium: The difference between the promised yields on a corporate bond and the yield on an otherwise identical government bond.

Default risk: The risk that the company issuing a bond may go bankrupt and default on its loans.

Derivatives: An asset whose value is derived from the price of another asset. Examples include call options, put options, futures and interest-rate swaps.

Dilutive merger: A merger in which the acquiring company's earnings per share decrease.

Discount rate: A rate that measures the risk of an investment. It can be understood as the expected return from a project of a certain amount of risk.

Discounted Cash Flow analysis (DCF): A method of valuation that takes the net present value of the free cash flows of a company.

Dividend: A payment by a company to shareholders of its stock, usually as a way to distribute some or all of the profits to shareholders.

EBIAT: Earnings Before Interest After Taxes. Used to approximate earnings for the purposes of creating free cash flow for a discounted cash flow.

EBIT: Earnings Before Interest and Taxes

EBITDA: Earnings Before Interest, Taxes, Depreciation and Amortization

Enterprise Value: Levered value of the company, the Equity Value plus the market value of debt.

Equity: In short, stock. Equity means ownership in a company that is usually represented by stock.

The Fed: The Federal Reserve Board, which gently (or sometimes roughly) manages the country's economy by setting interest rates.

Fixed income: Bonds and other securities that earn a fixed rate of return. Bonds are typically issued by governments, corporations and municipalities.

Float: The number of shares available for trade in the market times the price. Generally speaking, the bigger the float, the greater the stock's liquidity.

Floating rate: An interest rate that is benchmarked to other rates (such as the rate paid on U.S. Treasuries), allowing the interest rate to change as market conditions change.

Forward contract: A contract that calls for future delivery of an asset at an agreed-upon price.

Forward exchange rate: The price of currencies at which they can be bought and sold for future delivery.

Forward rates (for bonds): The agreed-upon interest rates for a bond to be issued in the future.

Futures contract: A contract that calls for the delivery of an asset or its cash value at a specified delivery or maturity date for an agreed upon price. A future is a type of forward contract that is liquid, standardized, traded on an exchange, and whose prices are settled at the end of each trading day.

Glass-Steagall Act: Part of the legislation passed during the Great Depression (Glass-Steagall was passed in 1933) designed to help prevent future bank failure – the establishment of the F.D.I.C. was also part of this movement. The Glass-Steagall Act split America's investment banking (issuing and trading securities) operations from commercial banking (lending). For example, J.P. Morgan was forced to spin off its securities unit as Morgan Stanley.

Goodwill: An account that includes intangible assets a company may have, such as brand image.

Hedge: To balance a position in the market in order to reduce risk. Hedges work like insurance: a small position pays off large amounts with a slight move in the market.

High-yield bonds (a.k.a. junk bonds): Bonds with poor credit ratings that pay a relatively high rate of interest.

Holding Period Return: The income earned over a period as a percentage of the bond price at the start of the period.

Income Statement: One of the four basic financial statements, the Income Statement presents the results of operations of a business over a specified period of time, and is composed of Revenues, Expenses and Net Income.

Initial Public Offering (IPO): The dream of every entrepreneur, the IPO is the first time a company issues stock to the public. "Going public" means more than raising money for the company; by agreeing to take on public shareholders, a company enters a whole world of required SEC filings and quarterly revenue and earnings reports, not to mention possible shareholder lawsuits.

Investment grade bonds: Bonds with high credit ratings that pay a relatively low rate of interest.

Leveraged Buyout (LBO): The buyout of a company with borrowed money, often using that company's own assets as collateral. LBOs were the order of the day in the heady 1980s, when successful LBO firms such as Kohlberg Kravis Roberts made a practice of buying up companies, restructuring them, and reselling them or taking them public at a significant profit. LBOs are now somewhat out of fashion.

Liquidity: The amount of a particular stock or bond available for trading in the market. Commonly traded securities such as large-cap stocks and U.S. government bonds are said to be highly liquid instruments. Small-cap stocks and smaller fixed income issues often are called illiquid (as they are not actively traded) and suffer a liquidity discount, i.e., they trade at lower valuations to similar, but more liquid, securities.

The Long Bond: The 30-year U.S. Treasury bond. Treasury bonds are used as the starting point for pricing many other bonds, because Treasury bonds are assumed to have zero credit risk, taking into account factors such as inflation. For example, a company will issue a bond that trades "40 over Treasuries." The 40 refers to 40 basis points (100 basis points = 1 percentage point).

Market Cap(italization): The total value of a company in the stock market (total shares outstanding x price per share).

Money market securities: This term is generally used to represent the market for securities maturing within one year. These include short-term CDs, Repurchase Agreements and Commercial Paper (low-risk corporate issues), among others. These are low risk, short-term securities that have yields similar to Treasuries.

Mortgage-backed bonds: Bonds collateralized by a pool of mortgages. Interest and principal payments are based on the individual homeowners making their mortgage payments. The more diverse the pool of mortgages backing the bond, the less risky they are.

Multiples method: A method of valuing a company that involves taking a multiple of an indicator such as price-to-earnings, EBITDA, or revenues.

Municipal bonds: Bonds issued by local and state governments, a.k.a. municipalities. Municipal bonds are structured as tax-free for the investor, which means investors in munis earn interest payments without having to pay federal taxes. Sometimes investors are exempt from state and local taxes, too. Consequently, municipalities can pay lower interest rates on muni bonds than other bonds of similar risk.

Net present value (NPV): The present value of a series of cash flows generated by an investment, minus the initial investment. NPV is calculated because of the important concept that money today is worth more than the same money tomorrow.

Non-convertible preferred stock: Sometimes companies issue non-convertible preferred stock, which remains outstanding in perpetuity and trades like stocks. Utilities represent the best example of non-convertible preferred stock issuers.

Par value: The total amount a bond issuer will commit to pay back when the bond expires.

P/E ratio: The price to earnings ratio. This is the ratio of a company's stock price to its earnings-per-share. The higher the P/E ratio, the more "expensive" a stock is (and also the faster investors believe the company will grow). Stocks in fast-growing industries tend to have higher P/E ratios.

Pooling accounting: A type of accounting used in a stock swap merger. Pooling accounting does not account for Goodwill, and is preferable to purchase accounting.

Prime rate: The average rate U.S. banks charge to companies for loans.

Purchase accounting: A type of accounting used in a merger with a considerable amount of cash. Purchase accounting takes Goodwill into account, and is less preferable than pooling accounting.

Put option: An option that gives the holder the right to sell an asset for a specified price on or before a specified expiration date.

Securities and Exchange Commission (SEC): A federal agency established as a result of the stock market crash of 1929 and the ensuing depression. The SEC monitors disclosure of financial information to stockholders, and protects against fraud. Publicly traded securities must first be approved by the SEC prior to trading.

Securitize: To convert an asset into a security that can then be sold to investors. Nearly any income-generating asset can be turned into a security. For example, a 20-year mortgage on a home can be packaged with other mortgages just like it, and shares in this pool of mortgages can then be sold to investors.

Selling, General & Administrative Expense (SG&A): Costs not directly involved in the production of revenues. SG&A is subtracted from Gross Profit to get EBIT.

Spot exchange rate: The price of currencies for immediate delivery.

Statement of Cash Flows: One of the four basic financial statements, the Statement of Cash Flows presents a detailed summary of all of the cash inflows and outflows during a specified period.

Statement of Retained Earnings: One of the four basic financial statements, the Statement of Retained Earnings is a reconciliation of the Retained Earnings account. Information such as dividends or announced income is provided in the statement. The Statement of Retained Earnings provides information about what a company's management is doing with the company's earnings.

Stock: Ownership in a company.

Stock swap: A form of M&A activity whereby the stock of one company is exchanged for the stock of another.

Strong currency: A currency whose value is rising relative to other currencies.

Swap: A type of derivative, a swap is an exchange of future cash flows. Popular swaps include foreign exchange swaps and interest rate swaps.

10K: An annual report filed by a public company with the Securities and Exchange Commission (SEC). Includes financial information, company information, risk factors, etc.

Tender offers: A method by which a hostile acquirer renders an offer to the shareholders of a company in an attempt to gather a controlling interest in the company. Generally, the potential acquirer will offer to buy stock from shareholders at a much higher value than the market value.

Treasury securities: Securities issued by the U.S. government. These are divided into Treasury bills (maturity of up to 2 years), Treasury notes (from 2 years to 10 years maturity) and Treasury bonds (10 years to 30 years). As they are government guaranteed, Treasuries are considered risk-free. In fact, while U.S. Treasuries have no default risk, they do have interest rate risk; if rates increase, then the price of USTs will decrease.

Underwrite: The function performed by investment banks when they help companies issue securities to investors. Technically, the investment bank buys the securities from the company and immediately resells the securities to investors for a slightly higher price, making money on the spread.

Weak currency: A currency whose value is falling relative to other currencies.

Yield to call: The yield of a bond calculated up to the period when the bond is called (paid off by the bond issuer).

Yield: The annual return on investment. A high-yield bond, for example, pays a high rate of interest.

Yield to maturity: The measure of the average rate of return that will be earned on a bond if it is bought now and held to maturity.

Zero coupon bonds: A bond that offers no coupon or interest payments to the bondholder.

Valuing a Company

Here, we'll take a look at the most common ways of assigning a market value to a company, also called valuation techniques.

Ratio Analysis

Equity analysts commonly use financial ratios as a way to value the stock of a company.   Specifically, they use ratios to analyze a company's past and present performance and predict future financial results. Generally, ratios are evaluated as a time series over the last few years, as a comparison against other industry competitors or as a comparison against benchmarks. Ratios are derived from line items on a company's financial statements (Balance Sheet, Income Statement and Statement of Cash Flows). Below are some common valuation measures used in evaluating companies in multiple industries.

Price Multiples	
Price to Earnings	Current stock price / Earnings per share
Price to Book	Current stock price / [assets – liabilities]
Price to Sales	Current stock price / Sales revenue
Price to Cash Flow	Current stock price / operating cash flow

Profitability Ratios	
Return on Sales	Net Income / Sales
Gross Margins	[Sales – Cost of Goods Sold] / Sales
Return on Assets (ROA)	[Net Income – After tax interest expense] / Average of the last two years' assets
Return on Equity (ROE)	Net income / Average of the last two years' total shareholders' equity

Balance Sheet Ratios

Asset Turnover	Sales / Average of the last two years' assets
Accounts Receivable (AR) Turnover	Sales / Average of the last two years' AR
Inventory Turnover	Cost of goods sold / Average of the last two years' inventory
Accounts Payable Turnover	This year's inventory purchases / Average of the last two years' accounts payable

Solvency Ratios

Financial Leverage	Total assets / Total shareholders' equity
Debt to Equity	Total debt / Total shareholders' equity

Discounted Cash Flow (DCF) Analysis

The DCF analysis has many variations, but it is simply a valuation exercise of projecting the cash flows of the company into the future (typically 5-7 years) and then discounting them to the present value using the company's cost of capital. This type of analysis is commonly taught in business schools and academic texts, but is not broadly used in the industry. Many opponents argue that predicting a terminal cash flow value and an appropriate discount rate are highly subjective and exposed to vast error. However, the concepts of a DCF analysis are often used in some form to evaluate investments. Below is a simplified approach to doing a discounted free cash flow analysis. Keep in mind this is a general outline and does not include many of the more detailed nuances of the analysis.

Step 1:

Calculate free cash flow for five to seven years in the future. Analysis is based on the financial projections made on the pro forma (predicted) balance sheet and income statement.

Calculating free cash flow

Net income
+ Depreciation expenses
+ Amortization of goodwill,
+ Year-over-year changes in deferred taxes
– Year-over year change in net working capital (current assets – current liabilities)
= Cash flow from operations

– Net capital expenditures
= Free cash flow

Step 2:

Determine the terminal value of free cash flows of the company when projections become too distant in the future to predict. In essence, you are assigning a constant growth rate for the company beyond the years that you can reasonable predict (typically 5 to 7 years).

Terminal Value = last year of projected free cash flows * (1+growth rate)

[The growth rate is usually based on the rate of inflation].

Step 3:

Discount each year's projected cash flow and the terminal value to the present time using the company's cost of capital (the weighted average of the company's cost of debt and the cost of equity).

Example of discounting 5 years of free cash flows

Year 1 Projected free cash flow / (1 + cost of capital)
+ Year 2 Projected free cash flow / $(1 + \text{cost of capital})^2$
+ Year 3 Projected free cash flow / $(1 + \text{cost of capital})^3$
+ Year 4 Projected free cash flow / $(1 + \text{cost of capital})^4$
+ Year 5 Projected free cash flow / $(1 + \text{cost of capital})^5$
+ Terminal value / $(1 + \text{cost of capital})^5$
───
= Total present discounted cash flow value

Step 4:

The discounted cash flow value is often referred to as the intrinsic value of the company. Analysts compare this intrinsic value to the stock market value of the company to determine whether the stock is over or under valued.

If Intrinsic Value > Stock Market Value, then the stock is undervalued (buy)

If Intrinsic Value < Stock Market Value, then the stock is overvalued (sell)

(For greater detail on valuation including more formulas, sample questions, and examples of the DCF analysis, see the *Vault Guide to the Finance Interviews*, the *Vault Guide to Advanced and Quantitative Finance Interviews*, and the *Vault Finance Interviews Practice Guide*.)

Want more practice with DCF analysis and other valuation techniques? Get expert Vault help.

- Insider guides, including the best-selling Vault Guide to Finance Interviews, the Vault Finance Interviews Practice Guide, the Vault Guide to Advanced and Quantitative Finance Interviews

- Vault's one-on-one Finance Interview Prep, a 1-hour live phone interview coaching session with a Vault expert

Go to the Vault Finance Career Channel at http://finance.vault.com

---

About the Author

Andrew R. Schlossberg: Andrew R. Schlossberg began his career in investment management in 1996 with Salomon Smith Barney Asset Management in New York. As an assistant vice president and equity research analyst, he worked with the U.S. investment team in the management of $12 billion in assets for institutional clients. After four years with Salomon, Mr. Schlossberg attended the Kellogg School at Northwestern University where he received a MBA with concentrations in Finance, Business Strategy, and Management of Organizations. Additionally, Mr. Schlossberg is the recipient of the Kellogg School Dean's Service Award and served as chairman of Kellogg's Student Admissions Committee and of the Global Initiatives in Management, Brazil course.

Currently, he is an associate in the executive development program of one of the world's largest asset management firms. In this role he participates in multiple investment and strategic business assignments throughout the global enterprise. He is a graduate of the University of Delaware (1996) and Kellogg Business School (2002).

Alexander Gorelik: Alexander Gorelik is currently a second-year MBA student at the University of Chicago. He most recently worked as an analyst at a hedge fund, researching equities in the software, Internet and telecom industries.